STRUCTURED INPUT

Grammar Instruction for the Acquisition-Oriented Classroom

The McGraw-Hill Second Language Professional Series

General Editors: James F. Lee and Bill VanPatten

Directions in Second Language Learning and Teaching

Primarily for students of second language acquisition and teaching, curriculum developers, and teacher educators, *Directions in Second Language Learning and Teaching* explores how languages are learned and used and how knowledge about language acquisition and use informs language teaching. The books in this strand emphasize principled approaches to classroom instruction and management as well as to the education of second language teachers.

Making Communicative Language Teaching Happen, Second Edition, 0-07-365517-1
by James F. Lee and Bill VanPatten

Translation Teaching: From Research to the Classroom, 0-07-248709-7
by Sonia Colina

Gender in the Language Classroom, 0-07-236749-0
by Monika Chavez

Tasks and Communicating in Language Classrooms, 0-07-231054-5
by James F. Lee

Affect in Foreign Language and Second Language Learning: A Practical Guide to Creating a Low-Anxiety Classroom Atmosphere, 0-07-038900-4
Edited by Dolly Jesusita Young

Communicative Competence: Theory and Classroom Practice, Second Edition, 0-07-083736-8
by Sandra J. Savignon

Beyond Methods: Components of Second Language Teacher Education, 0-07-006106-8
Edited by Kathleen Bardovi-Harlig and Beverly Hartford

Monographs in Second Language Learning and Teaching

The second strand in the series, *Monographs in Second Language Learning and Teaching,* is designed to provide brief and highly readable text for beginners and nonspecialists that can be used as supplements to any of the books in the *Directions* strand or with other main texts. An additional goal of the *Monographs* strand is to provide an array of short texts that instructors may combine in various ways to fashion courses that suit their individual needs.

Structured Input: Grammar Instruction for the Acquisition-Oriented Classroom, 0-07-288724-9
by Andrew P. Farley

Input Enhancement: From Theory and Research to the Classroom, 0-07-288725-7
by Wynne Wong

Teaching Writing in Second and Foreign Language Classrooms, 0-07-293479-4
by Jessica Willams

From Input to Output: A Teacher's Guide to Second Language Acquisition, 0-07-282561-8
by Bill VanPatten

Breaking Tradition: An Exploration of the Historical Relationship between Theory and Practice in Second Language Teaching, 0-07-044394-7
by Diane Musumeci

STRUCTURED INPUT

Grammar Instruction for the Acquisition-Oriented Classroom

Andrew P. Farley
University of Notre Dame

Boston   Burr Ridge, IL   Dubuque, IA   Madison, WI   New York
San Francisco   St. Louis   Bangkok   Bogotá   Caracas   Kuala Lumpur
Lisbon   London   Madrid   Mexico City   Milan   Montreal   New Delhi
Santiago   Seoul   Singapore   Sydney   Taipei   Toronto

The McGraw-Hill Companies

Higher Education

This is an book.

STRUCTURED INPUT: Grammar Instruction for the Acquisition-Oriented Classroom
Published by McGraw-Hill, a business unit of The McGraw-Hill Companies, Inc., 1221 Avenue of the Americas, New York, NY 10020. Copyright © 2005 by The McGraw-Hill Companies, Inc. All rights reserved. No part of this publication may be reproduced or distributed in any form or by any means, or stored in a database or retrieval system, without the prior written consent of The McGraw-Hill Companies, Inc., including, but not limited to, in any network or other electronic storage or transmission, or broadcast for distance learning.
Some ancillaries, including electronic and print components, may not be available to customers outside the United States.

This book is printed on acid-free paper.

1 2 3 4 5 6 7 8 9 0 BKM/BKM 0 9 8 7 6 5 4

ISBN 0-07-288724-9

Editor-in-chief: *Emily Barrosse*
Publisher: *William R. Glass*
Developmental editor: *Pennie Nichols*
Executive marketing manager: *Nick Agnew*
Project manager: *Mel Valentín*
Production supervisor: *Rich DeVitto*
Design manager: *Violeta Díaz*
Art editor: *Katherine McNab*
Designer: *Linda M. Robertson*
Compositor: *Precision Graphics*
Typeface: *Palatino*
Printer: *Bookmart Press*

Library of Congress Cataloging-in-Publication Data

Farley, Andrew P.
    Structured input: grammar instruction for the acquisition oriented classroom / Andrew P. Farley
        p. cm. --(McGraw-Hill second language professional series. Perspectives on theory and research)
    Includes bibliographical references and index.
    ISBN 0-07-288724-9 (pbk. ; alk. paper)
    1. Languages, Modern--Study and teaching 2. Second language acquisition I. Title. II.
Series

PB35.F35 2004
418'.0071--dc22   2004055970

When ordering this title, use ISBN 0-07-288724-9

www.mhhe.com

DEDICATION

. . . to my Father

CONTENTS

Foreword by James F. Lee/Bill VanPatten   x

Preface   xi

Key Terms and Their Acronyms   xv

CHAPTER *1*   *STRUCTURED INPUT: ADDRESSING LEARNERS'*
            PROCESSING STRATEGIES   1

Introduction   1

Input: A Brief History   1

What Is Input Processing?   5

What Is *Structured* Input?   11

Read More About It   17

CHAPTER *2*   *THE PRIMACY OF MEANING PRINCIPLE*   18

Introduction   18

Grammatical Forms Affected by Principle 1   19

The Primacy of Meaning: Some Research   20

Example 1: Future Tense in Italian   26

Example 2: Past Tense in German   33

Example 3: Subject-Verb Agreement in English   35

Principles in Practice   38

Three Sample Studies   39

Read More About It   41

CHAPTER 3 **THE SENTENCE LOCATION PRINCIPLE** 42

Introduction   42
Grammatical Forms Affected by P1f   43
The Sentence Location Principle: Some Research   44
Example 1: The Spanish Subjunctive   45
Example 2: The French *Avoir* + Negation   51
Principles in Practice   54
Two Sample Studies   55
Read More About It   57

CHAPTER 4 **THE FIRST NOUN PRINCIPLE** 58

Introduction   58
Grammatical Forms Affected by Principle 2   60
The First Noun Principle: Some Research   60
Example 1: Object Pronouns in Spanish   62
Example 2: Object Pronouns in German   67
Principles in Practice   71
Three Sample Studies   71
Read More About It   72

CHAPTER 5 **SI ACTIVITY DESIGN: COMMON PITFALLS AND FREQUENTLY ASKED QUESTIONS** 73

Introduction   73
Part 1: Common Pitfalls   73
Part 2: Frequently Asked Questions   85
Read More About It   91

CHAPTER 6 NEW RESEARCH ON SI 92

Introduction   92
Study 1: Farley and McCollam Wiebe
        Structured Input—Teaching the Unlearnable?   92
Study 2: Farley
        Learner Reactions to SI Activities On-Line   101
Final Remarks on Both Studies   107
Read More About It   108

Glossary   109
References   111
Index   116
About the Author   116

Since the first publications on processing instruction and structured input in the early 1990s, both practitioners and researchers alike have struggled with the nature of structured input activities. As the two researchers who are most associated with structured input, we have repeatedly been asked for additional and detailed work on this particular pedagogical intervention. Well, here it is.

In the present volume, Andrew Farley brings together theory, research, and practice on structured input in a clearly written exposition. True to the nature of the McGraw-Hill series, he makes both theoretical concepts and research accessible to the novice reader. Also true to the series, he makes the link between theory/research and practice, supplying the reader with abundant examples of structured input activities. Drawing on his own research as well as his own experience in teaching novice instructors about structured input, he has produced a solid volume that should satisfy those researchers and instructors who ask for more examples of and clarifications on structured input activities. His discussion of "pitfalls" in the development of structured input activities is especially welcome and provides valuable early feedback to activities creators.

To be sure, structured input may not be a technique that everyone embraces. This is true, however, of any pedagogical technique, method, or approach. But with this accessible presentation, readers can better decide if structured input will work for them or not. We thank Farley for this excellent contribution to the continued discussion of principled language instruction.

James F. Lee
Bill VanPatten

Many of us who teach Foreign Language Teaching Methodology courses are often bombarded with requests for examples illustrating the design of structured input (SI) activities for various language features. As they say, a picture is worth a thousand words. Even so, providing examples alone may only incite blind imitation of these activities and certainly will not bring about a thorough understanding of the theoretical underpinnings and the research findings that encourage use of SI. Hence, my motivations in writing this book are the following:

- To *familiarize* readers with what may be happening in learners' heads during on-line comprehension of aural and written input.
- To *present* instructors with the idea of structuring input to take advantage of these learner strategies or to encourage more optimal ones.
- To *analyze* existing research on SI that shows it to be a beneficial approach to focus-on-form.
- To *explain* and *illustrate* how effective SI activities can be designed using a variety of language features from five different languages.
- To *introduce* some of my new research on the effects of SI.

Through reading this book, language instructors and researchers alike will become comfortable with designing their own SI activities for second language (L2) classroom use and/or second language acquisition (SLA) studies. Although *Structured Input* was purposely written using language that requires little or no knowledge of contemporary SLA theory and/or research, it was designed to appeal to a variety of audiences including:

- *Graduate or undergraduate students* in a foreign language (FL) teaching methodology or SLA course who need to synthesize theoretical concepts and put them into practice.
- *Language instructors* at the high school or university level who may not have a background in SLA theory but wish to implement sound pedagogical techniques.

- *Faculty and administrators* who wish to become familiar with current understandings of how language learning happens and which types of instruction can be most effective.
- *SLA researchers* who want an up-to-date summary of current research, an introduction to some new research, and guidelines/examples for treatment design as they conduct replication studies.

Structured Input is organized into six chapters. Chapter 1 presents fundamental concepts in clear, easy-to-understand terms. Chapters 2 through 4 move from theoretical notions to research findings to the practice of SI activity design. These three middle chapters are identical in structure.

- Discussion of the processing principle(s) that is (are) in focus
- Some grammatical features affected by the principle(s)
- Research related to the principle(s)
- In-depth examples and discussion of activity design

Near the end of each of these chapters, a *Principles in Practice* section asks readers to design a series of activities that they can use in an upcoming class period with their students. Each of these chapters closes with a short reading list that includes SLA literature referred to within the chapter as well as additional sources of value to the reader.

Chapter 5 presents common pitfalls that activity designers may encounter as they attempt to fashion SI activities. The first set of pitfalls relates directly to *not* following specific guidelines for designing SI activities; the second set of pitfalls involves a misunderstanding of the nature and/or goals of SI activities. Finally, Chapter 5 addresses some frequently asked questions (FAQs) regarding SI activity design.

Chapter 6 presents the design, implementation, and results of two studies on the effects of SI activities. The first study focuses on low-intermediate learners and investigates whether SI can enable them to notice, process, and consequently produce language structures for which they are theoretically "unready." The second study presents learner feedback regarding the effectiveness and ease of use of on-line SI activities that were integrated into a university-level Spanish curriculum.

ACKNOWLEDGMENTS

First, I want to express my gratitude to James Lee and Bill VanPatten, General Editors of the McGraw-Hill Second Language Professional Series. I have always admired their ability to present theory and research in an easily digestible manner, and reading their work has helped me become a better academic writer.

Special thanks are due to Bill for reading the proposal and an early version of Chapter 3 (the sample chapter) and providing valuable feedback. He also gave me a few suggestions for improving Chapters 5 and 6. Bill was the reason that I decided to study SLA at University of Illinois at Urbana-Champaign, and without his model of input processing and groundbreaking research on the effects of processing instruction, this book simply would not exist. So many of us are indebted to him for the way that he has mentored us first as graduate students and later as research faculty. Here I only echo the thanks that he regularly receives from his students and other SLA colleagues.

I also want to recognize Michael Leeser and Elena Mangione-Lora for their help with translating some of the activity items into German and Italian. In addition, I want to convey gratefulness to Elena for the fine job that she did as Assistant Director of the Spanish Language Program at Notre Dame during the fall of 2003 when I was on sabbatical drafting this book. I also credit Kelly Kingsbury and Andrea Topash-Rios, who worked together with Elena to oversee the lower-level Spanish courses while I was on leave.

I want to thank William R. Glass, my publisher at McGraw-Hill in San Francisco. I have had the privilege of being involved with him on a few McGraw-Hill projects, and it is always a delight to work with him. In particular, I have enjoyed the freedom to be creative and his encouragement and praise during the process.

Thanks are also due to Pennie Nichols, the developmental editor, and to the Editorial, Design, and Production Team at McGraw-Hill: Project Manager Mel Valentín, Senior Production Supervisor Rich DeVitto, Senior Designer Violeta Díaz, and Editorial Assistant Stacy Shearer.

Several of my colleagues in SLA (Alessandro Benati, Wynne Wong, Bill VanPatten, and Teresa Cadierno) allowed me to include and/or modify SI activities that they had designed for their own use as instructional treatments. Their contributions enhanced Chapters 2, 3, and 4 a great deal, and I am indebted to them for their assistance. Special thanks go to Kristina McCollam-Wiebe, who permitted me to report in Chapter 6 on our recently completed study.

I want to express my appreciation to Marilyn Buck at UNAM in Mexico City, Gary Cziko at University of Illinois at Urbana-Champaign, and to the many other colleagues who sent e-mails and made phone calls to inquire about obtaining this book even before it went to press. Their interest in my work fueled my excitement about the readership that this book will enjoy around the United States and elsewhere.

I also wish to convey my gratitude to the reviewers who voiced their enthusiastic support for the publication of this book.

Joanne Burnett, University of Southern Mississippi

Kimberly L. Geeslin, Indiana University

Deborah Gill, Pennsylvania State University at Dubois

Lourdes Ortega, Northern Arizona University

This being my first book, I received quite a boost after reading their reviews. I am grateful for both their encouragement and their suggestions for improving the manuscript.

I want to thank my Department Chair Dayle Seidenspinner-Nuñez, Dean Mark Roche, and Associate Dean Gregory Sterling for approving my sabbatical leave and enabling me to complete this and other research projects during the 2003–2004 academic year. I am fortunate to be in an academic environment in which I feel respected and appreciated for my work.

I also want to credit several of my peers at Notre Dame: Colleen Ryan-Scheutz in Italian, Sebastien Dubreil in French, and Isabel Ferreira in Portuguese. I am lucky to have colleagues and friends like them, and I appreciate their co-teaching of our teaching methodology course while I was away writing this book.

Finally, I want to express my heartfelt gratitude to my wife, Katharine. Thank you for all of the emotional support that you gave me. I love you, and I am so excited to be spending this life-long adventure with you.

Andrew P. Farley
February 6, 2004

KEY TERMS AND THEIR ACRONYMS

EI	Explicit Information	PI	Processing Instruction
FNP	First Noun Principle	SI	Structured Input
GJT	Grammaticality Judgment Test	SLA	Second Language Acquisition
L1	First Language	SVO	Subject-Verb-Object
L2	Second Language	TI	Traditional Instruction
MOI	Meaning-Based Output Instruction	TPR	Total Physical Response
PDT	Picture Description Task	UG	Universal Grammar

CHAPTER 1

Structured Input: Addressing Learners' Processing Strategies

INTRODUCTION

How do classroom second language (L2) learners acquire new forms? Does instruction really make a difference? If so, what type of instruction is best? These are essential questions that deserve answers. Throughout this book I attempt to shed some light on these areas of inquiry. A majority of current researchers in second language acquisition (SLA) concur that instructional intervention can affect SLA, yet there is still debate about what *types* of instruction are most beneficial. Much of the debate relates to the respective roles of *input* and *output* in the creation of an implicit (unconscious) linguistic system in classroom L2 learners. Most, if not all, contemporary research has concluded that quality and quantity of input are the most important factors influencing whether SLA occurs or not. However, SLA researchers do not leave output out of the picture, and their findings indicate that output practice does bring about improvement on certain language tasks. Before we focus on the benefits of *structured* input (SI) in particular, first it is helpful to answer the question: Why is input so important?

> **DEFINITIONS**
>
> *Input:* linguistic data that a learner reads or hears and attends to for meaning.
>
> *Output:* oral or written language that a learner produces to express meaning.

INPUT: A BRIEF HISTORY

Even in pre-1970s behaviorism, which touted habit-formation as the avenue to SLA, we see input as the driving force of language acquisition. Although behaviorists did not ascribe to the idea that humans possess an innate set of language rules nor even an innate bent toward language learning, they still held that hearing input (and repeating after each utterance) brought about habits that resulted in SLA. Through behaviorism, we saw the rise of Audiolingualism in language teaching, which delivered substitution drills, transformations drills, and other similar pattern practicing to learners in hopes that a focus on form alone (rather than meaning) would solidify their knowledge and use of structures. Despite

1

the non-communicative nature of behavioristic approaches, even the behaviorist would state that without language stimuli (input) learners would be unable to arrive at language learning and use.

A decade after the rise of behaviorism, Krashen (1980, 1982) introduced his Input Hypothesis, suggesting that learners progressively acquire an L2 as they comprehend the *meaning* of input containing structures and forms that are just slightly above their current level of competence. Krashen radically departed from some traditional assumptions of his day when he proposed that learners attend to input for meaning first and consequently acquire the forms and structures of a language (see also Faerch and Kasper, 1986). Krashen stated the following:

> . . . our assumption has been that we first learn structures, then practice using them in communication, and this is how fluency develops. The input hypothesis says the opposite. It says we acquire by "going for meaning" first, and as a result, we acquire structure!

> (Krashen, 1982, p. 21)

We find evidence for Krashen's Input Hypothesis in that L2 learners who do not get *comprehensible* input, instead only raw (unaltered) input characteristic of native speakers, show little or no signs of acquiring the L2 except for perhaps the production of some unanalyzed chunks. Long (1981, 1983) points out that this phenomenon holds across studies of first and second language acquisition, by children and adults, in both normal and abnormal populations.

Pause to consider...

how you learned your second language. Are you able to discern the role that input had in your learning? What were the sources of input readily available to you? Did the classroom context (if applicable) supply you with a large quantity of input? Or was study abroad essential for you to really begin acquiring the language?

In the late eighties and early nineties, researchers began asking an important question regarding input—whether or not attention to form in the input was necessary for SLA to occur. Schmidt (1990, 1994), for example, held that *noticing*, a process beyond conscious registration, was a prerequisite for L2 acquisition and usage. Schmidt did not deny the existence of some incidental learning but argued that attention to form in the input is indispensable for L2 acquisition of certain features (namely, redundant forms). According to Schmidt, input cannot be "filtered" for further processing unless this process of noticing occurs first. Regardless of one's position on issues surrounding conscious attention, the fact remains that for more than a decade SLA researchers like Schmidt who have investigated attention issues have consistently operated under the assumption that input is essential to SLA.

Not only have many contemporary researchers articulated a central role for input, but theorists have constructed models and theories, all of which presume that input fuels the SLA process. Bates and MacWhinney's (1982, 1989)

Competition Model, for example, is based on the idea that acquisition is driven by "cues" in the input. Bates and MacWhinney contend for two levels of structure: a functional level in which meaning is expressed and a formal level in which surface forms appear. According to them, acquisition occurs when meaning is mapped to form—that is, when an interconnection is made from one level to the other. They argue that the connections made between meanings and forms have different relative strengths, and it is the nature of the input received that determines those strengths. Hence, L2 (or L1) processing involves competition among numerous cues in the input. Since input is what provides the cues in the Competition Model, it is therefore crucial for SLA to happen.

Probably the most cited linguist of all time, Noam Chomsky (1965) introduced the idea that humans are born with an innate linguistic system or grammar that "guides" them in language acquisition. According to Chomsky (1981), the evidence for these innate principles is the fact that children appear to unconsciously adhere to certain linguistic constraints within a given language that are entirely too abstract for them to deduce from the limited input they receive. Chomsky concludes that it could be only by the existence of an innate, underlying system (called Universal Grammar, or UG) that language learners attain a system that is not solely a reflection of the input they receive. Within Chomsky's framework, it is the *interaction* of input (albeit limited input) with these innate principles that results in acquisition. Certainly there is significant debate surrounding the relationship of UG to *second* language acquisition. While some researchers hold that L2 learners have no access to these universal principles, others argue that they may have partial or total access. The bottom line is that, if L2 learners have any access to UG at all, this access does them no good apart from the influx of input. Input is what causes learners to set (or reset for their L2) parameters for a particular language, and if the learner is not provided with input, these (re)settings will not occur.

This very brief overview of various perspectives on input and its place within some SLA theory and research is far from exhaustive. It serves only to demonstrate that contemporary SLA theorists and researchers are in accord that input is fundamental in order to acquire a second language. Despite the many theoretical approaches to SLA, the idea that learners require input remains consistent throughout. All agree that, without input, a learner's developing system will be halted and SLA cannot occur. Now that we have seen how important input is to SLA, we turn toward a theoretical model, VanPatten's (1996, 2004) Input Processing model, to address the following question: if input is essential for SLA to occur, then what *kind* of input is best for the L2 learner?

Pause to consider...

what kinds of input you think are best for learners. What are the characteristics of good input. Can you think of how unlearned forms might be highlighted in the input learners receive? How might this input be constructed?

A QUICK WORD ABOUT OUTPUT

Despite the obvious importance of input, this book does not advocate an input-only approach to foreign language (FL) instruction. Before we get too far into our investigation of structured input, let's see where output fits in. A number of theoretical frameworks and research studies have concluded that output plays a significant role in SLA. Let's take a brief look at what some SLA theorists and researchers have to say about the importance of output.

During the last decade and a half, Merrill Swain's Output Hypothesis (see Swain 1985, 1997) has sparked considerable interest in examining the effects of output practice on SLA. Swain's hypothesis is that language production *may* be a means of acquisition and that, without it, learners cannot achieve accuracy in the L2. This is largely due to the fact that producing utterances may cause learners to notice the aspects of their interlanguage that need further development. Swain purports that if the need is recognized, learners might pay more attention to L2 input. In addition, when learners are pushed to produce comprehensible output, this may spur the use of a new structure or form that they have never produced before.

In agreement with Swain, Gass (1997) states that output is fundamental to language learning operations in that it provides opportunity for hypothesis testing and feedback concerning hypotheses. Gass argues that producing language causes a type of proficiency at analysis that enables learners to string words and phrases together in new ways. Output also leads to both self-correction and feedback from others concerning the structures produced. VanPatten points out:

DEFINITIONS

Task Demands: what a particular L2 act requires of the learner.

Attentional Resources: the "space" available to learners in their working memory that enables storage of data during on-line comprehension.

Inner Speech: a "self talk" or interior rehearsing of what later becomes audible output.

> What Gass is arguing, it seems, is that interaction alters the task demands placed on a learner during input processing. The change in task demands frees up attentional resources allowing learners to process something they might miss otherwise. It must be made clear that this position **does not suggest that by producing the form in question during the interaction the learner is acquiring or has acquired the form;** the position is that by interacting the learner gets crucial data [input] from another interlocutor. (emphasis mine)
>
> —(VanPatten, 2004, p. 12)

In short, learners may realize that their output does not match the input they received during an interaction. This realization effect is the benefit that interaction brings for SLA.

Pica (1994) ascribes a major role to output in L2 interaction, arguing that it is negotiation by the listener and speaker that results in more comprehension. In addition, Pica states that requests for clarification during interaction often result in modification of the language produced. In other words, when linguistic demands placed on an L2 learner, it pushes him or her to produce comprehensible output. According to Pica, adjustments to an L2 learner's interlanguage can be accomplished by negotiated interaction with a native or another nonnative speaker. In summary, Pica's view is that output is necessary for negotiation, which in turn promotes more comprehension, and negotiated interaction helps to further interlanguage development.

Another important figure in current SLA theory hypothesized concerning the benefits of output practice long before Swain, Gass, or Pica. In 1962, the Soviet psychologist Lev Vygotsky put forth the output-related notion of "inner speech." He cited learning strategies such as mental rehearsal as types of inner speech and claimed that they serve as a covert (unseen) practicing of the L2. Vygotsky held that inner speech is not just a means of self-communication, rather it is a precursor to communicating with others. In the process of inner speech, speech mechanisms are activated without the audible manifestation of speech. In essence, output, although not externally evidenced, plays a fundamental role in the linguistic development of the L2 learner. This covert output practice moves toward subsequent stages of production and ultimately results in communication with others. We see then that Vygotskian Theory attributes a very significant role to output in SLA in that both covert (internalized) output and overt (externally evidenced) output are portrayed as fundamental processes in language development.

Although input is the fundamental requirement for SLA, we can readily see from many different theoretical angles that researchers have presented output as a crucial component. First, learners may not achieve accuracy without output practice, because producing utterances causes learners to notice deficiencies in their interlanguage. Second, output can lead to self-correction as well as feedback from others. Finally, output leads to negotiation by the listener and speaker that may ultimately result in more form-meaning connections. This happens because interaction makes input more processable since with interaction often comes shorter utterance length, circumlocution, repetition, and other processes that essentially free up attentional resources that are otherwise exhausted by the mere act of comprehension at the macro level ("getting the gist").

While this book does not provide a complete discussion of output and output-based instruction types, it does recognize the important role that output plays in classroom SLA. Keep in mind that successful structuring of an internal grammar in the L2 learner does not necessarily mean that the learner can create output with any degree of accuracy or fluency. Similarly, the mere fact that learners can engage in various types of output practice certainly does not mean that acquisition (successful form-meaning connections) is happening. Now that we have clearly established the value of output practice, let's continue with our look at input. We begin by investigating VanPatten's (1996, 2004) principles of input processing.

WHAT IS INPUT PROCESSING?

When we speak of input processing, we are referring only to one process among many in SLA. In addition to input being processed, learners' underlying knowledge (or internal grammar) is also being restructured, and learners also produce output. VanPatten's model of input processing does not address these latter two aspects of SLA. A framework like Chomsky's Universal Grammar seeks to define what is in learners' heads (in their developing system) that enables them to reset parameters, while a framework like Vygotskian Theory addresses the mechanisms or procedures involved in language production. Input Processing should be seen as complementary, not contradictory, to these other types of investigation into SLA since each framework addresses a different component of acquisition.

VanPatten's (1996, 2003) model of input processing addresses the specific issue of how intake, a subset of the input, is derived from input and which psycholinguistic strategies the L2 learner tends to rely on during input processing. We should be careful when we toss around terms like *processing*. Within VanPatten's model, processing takes place when a partial or total form-meaning connection has occurred during the act of comprehension. This simply means that an L2 learner has *noticed* a form and assigned meaning or grammatical function to it. Is it possible to notice a form but not process it? Absolutely. Many times, a learner may perceive the presence of a form but not be able to assign the form any meaning or function because his or her working memory is used up. In this case, processing (as we define it here) has not occurred. The portion of the input that does get processed and is then a candidate for integration into the learner's developing system is called *intake*. Note that although a form becomes part of the intake it will not automatically "stick" in the *developing system*. It may take a number of instances of noticing and (partial) processing before the form or structure is integrated. Specific strategies that L2 learners rely on during processing were introduced in VanPatten (1996) and recently revised in VanPatten (2004) in the form of two basic principles, each having a number of subprinciples. In this chapter, we briefly examine each principle and its corresponding subprinciples. In the following chapters, we look at VanPatten's principles in more depth. For now, we begin with a look at Principle 1, the Primacy of Meaning Principle.

> **DEFINITIONS**
>
> *Processing:* when partial or total form-meaning connections occur.
>
> *Noticing:* the simple act of recognizing that a feature exists.
>
> *Intake:* processed input that may or may not enter the developing system.
>
> *Developing system:* the term used to describe where a learner's form-meaning connections are stored.

Principle 1.   The Primacy of Meaning Principle. *Learners process input for meaning before they process it for form.*

P1a. *The Primacy of Content Words Principle.* Learners process content words in the input before anything else.

P1b. *The Lexical Preference Principle.* Learners will tend to rely on lexical items as opposed to grammatical form to get meaning when both encode the same semantic information.

P1c. *The Preference for Nonredundancy Principle.* Learners are more likely to process nonredundant meaningful grammatical form before they process redundant meaningful forms.

P1d. *The Meaning-before-Nonmeaning Principle.* Learners are more likely to process meaningful grammatical forms before nonmeaningful forms irrespective of redundancy.

P1e. *The Availability of Resources Principle.* For learners to process either redundant meaningful grammatical forms or nonmeaningful forms, the processing of overall sentential meaning must not drain available processing resources.

P1f. The Sentence Location Principle. Learners tend to process items in sentence initial position before those in final position and those in medial position.

VanPatten (2004)

Principle 1 *The Primacy of Meaning Principle. Learners process input for meaning before they process it for form.*

This principle is certainly generalizable to first language learning and even native-native interactions. However, what makes it so significant for L2 learners is that they often do not have enough attentional resources to process form. That is, when meaning and form are in competition for storage in their working memory, it will be form that is always second choice, and many times there will not be any "room" left.

P1a. Learners process content words in the input before anything else.

This subprinciple, called the Primacy of Content Words Principle, basically answers the following question: *where* do learners look for meaning first? The answer is content words. From their L1 experience, L2 learners are certainly aware that not all words in an utterance are of the same nature. They know that some words will help gather the essential meaning conveyed, while other words are simply "fillers." While it is true that sometimes these filler words are processed together with other sentential elements as unanalyzed chunks, for the most part L2 learners naturally (*not* by conscious choice) filter out words that simply serve as grammatical markers and focus on content words during comprehension. L2 learners may take advantage of their L1 experience from an acoustic perspective as well. In general, they realize that content words are more acoustically salient than are other sentential elements, and this results in learners looking for acoustic hints as to where to find the essential meaning in an oral utterance.

P1b. Learners will tend to rely on lexical items as opposed to grammatical form to get meaning when both encode the same semantic information.

This principle, termed the Lexical Preference Principle, involves a competition for learners' resources when there are redundant features in an input string. In many cases, two or more elements in an utterance or a discourse will communicate the same thing. For example, in the utterance *Yesterday Leslie played tennis at the YMCA,* both the lexical item *yesterday* and the *-ed* verb ending communicate past tense. The Lexical Preference Principle states that, in this instance, learners will naturally tend to rely on *yesterday* over the verb inflection in order to gather semantic information (when the action is occurring). The obvious disadvantage to this learner strategy is that it will hinder learners from processing the past tense marker since they do not need to process it to comprehend the utterance. Indeed, they may even perceive the presence of the marker (visually or aurally) yet still not process it due to the limits of their working memory. This is only one example of *redundancy.* Later, we will see how this principle interacts with grammatical points in a number of languages.

DEFINITIONS

Redundancy: when two or more elements in an utterance or discourse encode the same semantic information.

P1c. Learners are more likely to process nonredundant meaningful grammatical form before they process redundant meaningful forms.

This principle, The Preference for Nonredundancy Principle, logically follows from the preceding discussion. When an input string presents two or more grammatical forms, learners will naturally "gravitate" toward processing the nonredundant form(s). Again, this stems from the fact that they will not *need* to process the redundant L2 feature to comprehend the utterance or discourse. Thus, learners process on a need basis—do they need to process a given form to arrive at the meaning of a message? If so, their working memory will make an attempt. If they do not need the element processed for meaning, they most likely will not process it, since another element exists (a lexical item) that was sufficient to deliver the necessary semantic information.

P1d. Learners are more likely to process meaningful grammatical forms before nonmeaningful forms irrespective of redundancy.

This Meaning-Before-Nonmeaning Principle is easily understood. When two forms are in competition to be processed, what chiefly determines which form will be processed is the meaning (or lack of meaning) that each form carries. Regardless of whether or not one or both forms are redundant, the form carrying semantic information will more likely be processed before the form that does not convey meaning. When one looks at P1c and P1d in conjunction, it becomes apparent that there is a hierarchy of processability from most likely to least likely, as shown in Table 1.1.

Keep in mind that morphology is not the only way in which meaning is delivered. Syntax (the given word order of an utterance) can also play a significant role, and this will be particularly evident as we look at the next main principle, Principle 2.

P1e. For learners to process either redundant meaningful grammatical forms or nonmeaningful forms, the processing of overall sentential meaning must not drain available processing resources.

This subprinciple, called the Availability of Resources Principle, states that with an increase in utterance comprehensibility comes an increased probability that a form in that given utterance will be processed. Again, all these subprinciples (P1e included) stem from the notion that working memory is limited and the act of real-time comprehension uses up those resources. Hence, P1e is saying that if a learner can understand the rest of a sentence fairly easily, there will be resources left over for processing a new form in that

TABLE 1.1 Processing Difficulties Based on Redundancy and Meaningfulness

	Redundant?	Meaningful?
Least likely	Yes* or No	No
More likely	Yes	Yes
Most likely	No	Yes

*Note: It is difficult to find an instance of a redundant, nonmeaningful form.

utterance. Individual learner variables such as level of proficiency (beginner, intermediate, advanced) and degree of familiarity with particular lexical items will naturally affect how drained a learner's resources become during comprehension.

P1f. Learners tend to process items in sentence initial position before those in final position and those in medial position.

The Sentence Location Principle lays out a specific hierarchy with regard to the likelihood that L2 features will be processed. I use the utterance *John hates movies* to illustrate each utterance position with an example:

Most Difficult	Utterance-medial items	*hate -s*
Difficult	Utterance-final items	*movie -s*
Least Difficult	Utterance-initial items	*John*

In this simple utterance, P1f (not considering other potential factors) would predict that processing the meaning and function of *John* as subject would be the least difficult. In addition, the third person singular marker *-s* on the verb would be more difficult to process than the *-s* plural marker on *movies*. Of course, this is only one utterance, and a learner would normally need many input strings in order to begin noticing and subsequently processing either marker. In addition, there may certainly be other factors at play (utterance length, for example) in processing these features. However, for the sake of the present discussion, we can see that L2 processors are sensitive to position within an utterance. The easiest forms to process are those located in initial position within an utterance, as is the case with *John*. The second easiest forms to process occur in utterance-final position, as does *movie -s*. The most difficult forms to process are those that occur in utterance-medial position. You may know an L2 learner of English who has been studying English a long time but still produces oral utterances such as *John hate movies*. Which marker was noticed, processed, integrated in their developing system, and produced? Which one was not? Most likely, the plural *-s* marker has been integrated into their developing system, while the third person singular verb ending has not. We see here the influence of P1f as well as P1b (the Lexical Preference Principle), since the verbal marker *-s* simply recommunicates that *John* is the "hater" of movies.

Principle 2   The First Noun Principle. Learners tend to process the first noun or pronoun they encounter in a sentence as the subject/agent.

> P2a. *The Lexical Semantics Principle.* Learners may rely on lexical semantics, where possible, instead of word order to interpret sentences.
> P2b. *The Event Probabilities Principle.* Learners may rely on event probabilities, where possible, instead of word order to interpret sentences.
> P2c. *The Contextual Constraint Principle.* Learners may rely less on the First Noun Principle if preceding context constrains the possible interpretation of a clause or sentence.
>
> VanPatten (2004)

Principle 2   The First Noun Principle. Learners tend to process the first noun or pronoun they encounter in a sentence as the subject/agent.

Research on sentence-level processing indicates that beginning-level L2 learners assign the role of subject (or agent) to the first noun or pronoun that they encounter in an utterance. This means that an ESL learner might interpret *John was adored by his father* as *John adored his father.* This phenomenon (the first noun principle) is not merely a product of L1 interference. Rather, it is evidenced among L2 learners whose native language mandates SVO (subject-verb-object) word order *and* other L2 learners whose L1 allows OVS as well. As we will see in a later chapter, the first noun principle can affect the acquisition of various language features, including (but not limited to) object pronouns, case markers, and passive constructions.

P2a. Learners may rely on lexical semantics, where possible, instead of word order to interpret sentences.

The Lexical Semantics Principle cites one instance in which the First Noun Principle can be overridden. When we first introduced Principle 2 above, we looked at the sentence *John was adored by his father.* Recall that L2 learners can tend to interpret this sentence as *John adored his father.* But what if the utterance was *Golf was adored by his father* instead? Do you think learners would exhibit the same tendency to interpret *golf* as the agent? Probably not, since lexical semantics (here, the inanimate nature of golf) plays a role in this second utterance. This is what is meant by the Lexical Semantics Principle.

P2b. Learners may rely on event probabilities, where possible, instead of word order to interpret sentences.

Now, let us replace *golf* in the preceding example with an animate object such as *the parrot,* and consider the following sentence: *The parrot was adored by John's father.* This utterance now contains two animate objects (*parrot* and *John's father*), yet this utterance is less likely to be misinterpreted than the original utterance *John was adored by his father.* This is because the Event Probabilities Principle has come into play—it is slightly more difficult to imagine a parrot adoring someone than it is to imagine John adoring someone.

P2c. Learners may rely less on the First Noun Principle if preceding context constrains the possible interpretation of a clause or sentence.

Sometimes it is neither lexical semantics nor event probabilities that attenuate the First Noun Principle (FNP), yet the FNP is still overridden. A third cause for this is what is known as the Contextual Constraint Principle, which highlights the role that context can play in sentence-level processing. To be specific, contextual information (versus a lack of context) can have a significant effect on how learners process clauses containing OVS word order. L2 learners' tendency to rely on the First Noun Principle is lessened when processing utterances that have constraining contexts. In fact, some L2 learners do not exhibit any tendencies to employ the FNP at all when utterances are accompanied by constraining contexts.

Pause to consider . . .

how these L2 learner strategies affect the processing of features in the language(s) that you teach. Can you think of any forms that might not be processed because of Principle 1 or 2 or any of the subprinciples?

Before we look at how a language instructor can take these learner-processing strategies into account during activity design, it is important to note that VanPatten's (1996, 2004) principles are not the product of mere speculation. At one time, it is true, each of these principles and subprinciples was only a hypothesis. However, a significant body of SLA (and first language acquisition) research has since confirmed that each principle is psycholinguistically valid. That is, language learners are indeed doing these things. Of course, at present, some of the principles have been investigated and validated more than others. Still, there is overwhelming consensus among studies carried out by a variety of researchers that these tendencies exist. The only questions that remain are to what degree they are employed and what instructional interventions can alter or inhibit these tendencies. This is precisely where structured input will come into play. This book is divided in such a way that P1a–e are treated in Chapter 2, P1f in Chapter 3, and P2a–c in Chapter 4. Although the research that lends support to the psycholinguistic validity of these principles is spread out over three chapters, Table 1.2 offers a summary list of the principles along with the cited studies that lend support to them.

We will not review all the research studies supporting the principles now, but you should be aware that there are a significant number of empirical studies that led to VanPatten's positing of Principles 1 and 2.

TABLE 1.2 A Summary of Research Supporting Principles 1 and 2

Number	Principle	Empirical Evidence
Principle 1	Primacy of Meaning	Klein (1986); VanPatten (1990);
P1a	Primacy of Content Words	Mangubhai (1991); Bardovi-Harlig
P1b	Lexical Preference	(1992); Lee, Cadierno, Glass, &
P1c	Preference for Nonredundancy	VanPatten (1997); Glass (1994);
P1d	Meaning-Before-Nonmeaning	Musumeci (1989); Bransdorfer
P1e	Availability of Resources	(1989); Bransdorfer (1991); Berne (1992); Blau (1990).
P1f	Sentence Location	Barcroft & VanPatten (1997); Rosa & O'Neill (1998); Kim (1995).
Principle 2	First Noun	Nam (1975); Ervin-Tripp (1974); VanPatten (1984); Glisan (1985); Lee (1987b); LoCoco (1987); Binkowski 1992); Gass (1989); McDonald & Heilenman (1992); Pléh (1989).
P2a	Lexical Semantics	Bavin & Shopen (1989);
P2b	Event Probabilities	Issidorides & Hulstijn (1992);
P2c	Contextual Constraint	VanPatten & Houston (1998)

WHAT IS STRUCTURED INPUT?

Structured input (SI) is based on VanPatten's (1996, 2004) model of input processing and the principles outlined therein. SI activities purposely take into account the interpretation strategies (Principles 1 and 2) of the learner. That is, SI activities are a deliberate attempt to push the learners to notice and subsequently process target forms that might otherwise go unnoticed. At no time is the learner required to produce the target item during an SI activity; rather, the focus is entirely on the interpretation of preformed utterances or portions of utterances that are structured to benefit the learner more than raw (unstructured) input. VanPatten (1996) proposes six guidelines for the successful design of SI activities.

A. Present one thing at a time.

This guideline refers to the number of forms that an instructor presents to a learner in one activity. If our goal is to have L2 learners make correct form-meaning connections, then how is that best achieved? Guideline A suggests the simplest, most economical route—present them with one new form-meaning connection at a time. With only one new form to attend to, learners will be more likely to actually map meaning onto that form. In contrast, if learners are required to process multiple new forms at once, most likely one or more of those forms will go unnoticed. A secondary benefit of the one-at-a-time approach is that the explicit information given to students (grammar explanation, hints for processing, examples, and so on) is kept to a minimum. This helps prevent the classroom dynamic from taking a turn toward being a "grammar lecture." One cannot underestimate the value that a brief (rather than lengthy) introduction to a grammar point holds when an instructor is trying to keep a language course lively and interesting. By focusing on one form at a time, the instructor is able to launch immediately into meaningful topics that provide context for the targeted form.

To illustrate how effective this approach to grammar instruction can be, we will use an example from Spanish. Imagine that an instructor wants to present the past tense (preterit) forms to an introductory Spanish class. This class hour might begin with the instructor simply stating that the day's focus would be on *individuos famosos del pasado* (famous individuals of the past). The instructor might then mention that *Cristóbal Colón* (Christopher Columbus), saying that he . . .

...*ganó el favor de reyes.*	. . . won the favor of kings.
...*salió de su propio país.*	. . . left his own country.
...*«descubrió» el Nuevo Mundo.*	. . . "discovered" the New World.
...*regresó a España como héroe.*	. . . returned to Spain a hero.

In the process, the instructor might jot down these short statements for students to see. They have now heard and read four past tense utterances about Christopher Columbus. The instructor then transitions by saying, "Now we are going to look at other famous individuals from the past. Activity A is about . . ." This launches the class into a series of SI activities that exclusively introduces learners to more third person singular forms. From there, students move on to output-based activities in which they get to tell about interesting historical figures and what they accomplished to become famous.

Notice how the contextualized "story" about the instructor's choice of historical figure took the place of a traditional grammatical explanation. Was meaning kept in focus? Absolutely. Were students still exposed to the new forms? Yes. Underlining or circling the verb endings is a quick and easy way to further highlight the forms while still avoiding a lengthy grammar explanation. Presenting one thing at a time makes all of this work well.

Pause to consider . . .

a story you might tell for future tense in the language that you teach. To what grammatical form (person and number) would you limit the first set of activities? What topic or theme would you select for your input presentation ("story")?

B. Keep meaning in focus.

Examine Activity A for a moment, and ask yourself: is meaning kept in focus with this activity? Determining whether meaning is kept in focus during an activity is really quite simple. One must ask only this: can learners complete this activity without understanding what they hear or read? If so, then meaning is not kept in focus. In Activity A, it is certainly possible that learners listen for the past tense -*d* endings (or other past forms) and write those words down without understanding the discourse as a whole. In addition, the fact that in Activity A learners are instructed to listen only for form (and a limited number of forms, to be specific) shows just how mechanical this activity really is. Much like a secretary takes dictation, learners here are simply writing down what they hear, and the meaning of the message is almost irrelevant. In contrast, look at an alternative in Activity B to see how meaning can be kept in focus.

Activity A   Richard's Weekend

Listen to Richard tell about his weekend, and write down the four past tense verb forms that you hear.

Past Tense Forms:

1. _____   3. _____
2. _____   4. _____

INSTRUCTOR'S SCRIPT

My weekend was really relaxed. I just went out once to visit a friend at his apartment. Other than that, I stayed up late every night watching movies I rented and shopping for a new tennis racket on eBay. I finished all my homework on Friday, so I played around most of the weekend. I called my parents on Sunday just to check up on the new house they are building. All in all, it was a pretty low-key weekend.

Activity B Richard's Weekend

Read the following statements that Richard made about his weekend and decide which ones are similar to your own activities last weekend.

Richard . . .

_____ 1. . . . called his family.

_____ 2. . . . visited a friend at his apartment.

_____ 3. . . . stayed up past midnight every night.

_____ 4. . . . finished all his homework on Friday.

If learners are to successfully complete this activity, truly relating Richard's weekend to their own weekend, then they must understand the meaning of each utterance. In this sense, in contrast to Activity A, meaning is kept in focus. This communicates to learners that what they understand and how they respond to content in class not only matter but directly contributes to the success of classroom tasks.

C. Move from sentences to connected discourse.

During the initial stages of exposure to a form, learners will struggle even more if utterances are not kept short. Lengthier utterances tend to exhaust learners' working memory and do not allow any "leftover" for processing a new form. For this reason, instructors should pay special attention to the activity items that they create for learners' initial exposure to a structure. At the same time, it is important that learners be exposed to connected discourse during a lesson. However, the connected discourse format should be delayed until learners have had adequate opportunity to notice and process the new form. As a general guideline, it is best to move from shorter utterances (perhaps the first two to three activities) to more lengthy utterances (the next one to two activities) and then to connected discourse (the next one to two activities) before moving on to output-focused activities. What would an activity with connected discourse look like? Pulling from the "Richard's weekend" theme, Activity C serves as an example.

Activity C Richard's Weekend

Listen to the following story that Richard told about his weekend and decide which statements accurately describe what happened. Indicate T (true) or F (false).

Richard . . .

_____ 1. . . . viewed some films.

_____ 2. . . . went to a big party.

_____ 3. . . . completed some repairs.

_____ 4. . . . relaxed most of the weekend.

INSTRUCTOR'S SCRIPT
My weekend was really relaxed. I just went out once to visit a friend at his apartment. Other than that, I stayed up late every night watching movies I rented and shopping for a new tennis racket on eBay. I finished all my homework on Friday, so I played around most of the weekend. I called my parents on Sunday just to check up on the new house they are building. All in all, it was a pretty low-key weekend.

D. Use both oral and written input.

Some learners have difficulty learning new forms without having the opportunity to read them—that is, to see what they look like. Hearing the forms allows only for sound-meaning connections, whereas written form-meaning connections are made via reading. Instructors should make concerted efforts to provide their learners with both types of input, both for variety's sake and to appeal to different styles of learning that potentially exist in their classroom.

E. Have learners do something with the input.

This is what differentiates SI *activities* from just giving learners input. Learners need to be pushed to make decisions based on meaning and form instead of being mere recipients of input. What learners are required to do with the input may be different from one activity to the next. For example, some activities are based on a binary option, requiring learners to decide whether statements are true/false or likely/unlikely. Matching activities may require learners to make a logical connection between an input string and a photo, drawing, famous person, or vocabulary item. Information gap activities require learners to supply information related to the input they are given without producing the targeted form itself. Finally, some activities are of a multiple-choice nature and provide three or more possible alternatives. The learners are required to select the answer that best completes each sentence or corresponds best with each activity item given.

F. Keep the learner's processing strategies in mind.

Activities that merely provide meaning-bearing input and have learners make decisions still do not qualify as SI activities. Perhaps the most important guideline of all is to *keep the learner's processing strategies in mind.* Earlier in this chapter, you were exposed to all of VanPatten's principles of input processing. Guideline F states that it is important to take into account what is happening in the learner's head during the act of input processing. We saw, for example, that learners have difficulty processing a form that is in the middle of an utterance. To "keep this in mind" would mean that, in some instances, an instructor might purposefully move a new form to the beginning of each activity item to make it more salient and therefore more likely to be processed. Just a moment ago, you examined some true/false items in Activity C about Richard's weekend. Did you notice that "Richard" was pulled out and separated from the utterances listed? In this way, the past tense forms were placed at the beginning of each activity item. This is just one example of keeping a learner's processing strategies in mind.

TABLE 1.3 VanPatten's Guidelines for SI Activity Design

	Refers to:
(a) Present one thing at a time.	Single activity
(b) Keep meaning in focus.	Single activity
(c) Move from sentences to connected discourse.	Whole lesson
(d) Use both oral and written input.	Whole lesson
(e) Have learners do something with the input.	Single activity
(f) Keep the learner's processing strategies in mind.	Single activity

TABLE 1.4 Some Research on Structured Input

Study on PI / SI	Language Feature	Assessment Tasks & Results
VanPatten & Cadierno (1993)	Spanish: object pronouns	Interpretation: PI > TI Production: PI = TI
Cadierno (1995)	Spanish: preterit tense	Interpretation: PI > TI Production: PI = TI
Cheng (1995)	Spanish: *ser* and *estar*	Interpretation: PI > TI Production: PI = TI

VanPatten & Sanz (1995)	Spanish: object pronouns	Oral Production:
		  PI group improved
		  significantly

VanPatten & Oikennon (1996)	Spanish: object pronouns	Interpretation: PI = SI Production: PI = SI
Buck (2000)	ESL: present continuous	Interpretation: PI > TI Production: PI = TI
Benati (2001)	Italian: future tense	Interpretation: PI > TI Written Production: PI = TI Oral Production: PI = TI
Farley (2001a)	Spanish: subjunctive mood	Interpretation: PI > MOI Production: PI = MOI
Farley (2001b)	Spanish: subjunctive mood	Interpretation: PI = MOI Production: PI = MOI
Benati (2004)	Italian: future tense	Interpretation: PI = SI Production: PI = SI
Farley (2004a)	Spanish: regular, irregular, and novel subjunctives	Interpretation: PI = MOI Production: PI = MOI
Wong (2004)	French 'de' with 'avoir'	Interpretation: PI = SI Production: PI = SI

TI = Traditional Instruction

MOI = Meaning-Based Output Instruction

SI = Structured Input Only (no explicit information)

PI = Processing Instruction

We have just examined all six of VanPatten's (1996) guidelines for SI activity design. Four of the guidelines are requirements for individual SI activities, while two guidelines refer to an entire lesson. In other words, a lesson containing numerous activities should move from sentences to connected discourse and provide both oral and written input.

Throughout the next few chapters, we will look in detail at how to design activities that attempt either to alter Principles 1 and 2 or to take advantage of them. We will also look at a number of empirical studies that have investigated the effects of SI activities. Before we move on to Chapter 2, it will be helpful to have an overview of what this body of research communicates to teaching practitioners about SI. Table 1.4 summarizes the results of a number of studies on SI.

The most encouraging news about these studies is the fact that, in every case, the groups that received SI activities always did as well as but most often outperformed the output-focused group on two types of tasks: interpretation and production. In other words, the worst critique that one could make about SI activities is that, in some instances, they seem to bring about only as much improvement as (but not more than) some types of output-focused instructional materials. To date, there has been no empirical study in which the output-based treatment led to *greater* overall gains than did the group that received SI activities. These findings reveal the crucial role of input in SLA and the benefits of structuring input to help learners notice the form, process it, and acquire it. Of course, as we have underscored already, this does not mean that output is unimportant or that it should be de-emphasized in the foreign language classroom. Rather, it simply means that providing learners with SI is an effective way of introducing and "practicing" grammatical structures, especially when a grammatical feature may otherwise go undetected and/or unprocessed due to a learner processing problem.

Now that you have had a surface-level introduction to VanPatten's (2004) principles of input processing, the guidelines for SI activity design, and some of the research, the next few chapters will serve to deepen your understanding of these concepts.

READ MORE ABOUT IT

Lee, J., & VanPatten, B. (2003). *Making communicative language teaching happen* (2d ed.). New York: McGraw-Hill.

VanPatten, B. (1996). *Input processing and grammar instruction: Theory and research*. Norwood, NJ: Ablex.

VanPatten, B. (2003). *From input to output: A teacher's guide to second language acquisition*. New York: McGraw-Hill.

VanPatten, B., ed. (2004). *Processing instruction: Theory, research, and commentary*. Mahwah, NJ: Erlbaum.

CHAPTER 2

The Primacy
of Meaning Principle

INTRODUCTION

Imagine that you are learning English. Take a minute to examine the following utterances:

(1) Last night we walked along the beach.
(2) Tomorrow I will take you out to dinner.
(3) I always make an effort to be on time.

Would you be able to tell whether each of these sentences was referring to the past, present, or future *without* knowing the forms that mark tense in English? If so, how would you know? There is indeed a clue in each of the utterances above—*last night, tomorrow,* and *always*. If you are like a majority of L2 learners of English, you tend to look to these lexical clues before looking elsewhere (verb forms or endings) to determine when the action is occurring. You may not even notice, much less process, the *-ed* verb ending, the *will* future marker, or the present form *make* (versus *made*) if you have already processed the lexical time markers. This tendency to depend on lexical items over grammatical markers when they both encode the same meaning is certainly less than optimal in that it hinders the acquisition of certain L2 features.

In this chapter, we look at VanPatten's (2004) Primacy of Meaning Principle, which states that learners process input for meaning before they process it for form. This principle helps explain why forms that recommunicate semantic information already expressed elsewhere in the utterance may not be noticed, or may be noticed but not subsequently processed, by L2 learners. This tendency to process meaning before form exists because learners' working memory has a limited capacity for processing, and learners are therefore *forced* to privilege certain items (such as the time- and frequency-related phrases above) over others that express the same information. That is, their L2 processor is instinctively motivated to extract the communicative intent of the speaker or writer.

Romance languages interact with Principle 1 in similar ways, as you can see from Table 2.1, while English and German are affected in slightly different ways. In Spanish, French, and Italian, we see tense, aspect, and mood are marked morphologically, yet they also may be "marked" (communicated) by lexical items such as *ayer* 'yesterday' (Spanish) or *domani* 'tomorrow' (Italian), or *régulièrement* 'regularly' (French) for tense.

As for aspect, adverbial expressions meaning *one time, normally,* and so on may communicate the subtleties of aspect that are also marked morphologically in the verb endings. In Spanish for example, if one hears *De vez en cuando hablaba con mi mamá* (From time to time I spoke [imperfective aspect] with my mom) it will not be necessary to attend to the *-aba* verb ending in order to extract the aspectual meaning of the utterance. Since the expression *De vez en cuando...* (From time to time . . .) already expresses the idea that the action was ongoing and somewhat habitual, the need to differentiate between perfective and imperfective morphology during utterance comprehension is nonexistent. We see this in English and German as well as in Romance and other languages.

When mood is marked morphologically, learners will still tend to process lexical items that encode the same semantic information. For example, when the subjunctive mood in Romance is used to express emotion or uncertainty, learners will tend to process accompanying expressions meaning *I am happy that . . .* , *I hate that . . .* , *I doubt that . . .*, and so on rather than attending to the verbal morphology to obtain this meaning. In the case of expressions of emotion, we see only a partial redundancy. That is, the verb ending recommunicates that emotion is expressed, but it does not mark whether the emotion is

TABLE 2.1

Examples of Grammatical Forms Affected by Principle 1

Spanish	French	Italian	English (ESL)	German
Tense markers when adverbials of time are present	Tense markers when adverbials of time are present	Tense markers when adverbials of time are present	Tense markers when adverbials of time are present	Tense markers when adverbials of time are present
Subject-verb agreement when explicit subjects are present	Subject-verb agreement when explicit subjects are present	Subject-verb agreement when explicit subjects are present	Subject-verb agreement	Subject-verb agreement when explicit subjects are present
Aspectual markers when adverbials of aspect are present	Aspectual markers when adverbials of aspect are present	Aspectual markers when adverbials of aspect are present	Aspectual markers when adverbials of aspect are present	Aspectual markers when adverbials of aspect are present
Mood when expressions of uncertainty or emotion are present	Mood when expressions of uncertainty or emotion are present	Mood when expressions of uncertainty or emotion are present		

positive or negative in nature. Nor does the verbal marker indicate the relative strength of the emotion expressed. With uncertainty, we see a stronger redundancy in that there do not exist two types of uncertainty that are polar opposites. Rather, there are only subtle degrees of uncertainty. Hence, subjunctive markers in Romance languages at times are recommunicating uncertainty already expressed elsewhere (lexically), although the morphology alone can never communicate the *degree* of uncertainty. The point in both cases (emotion and uncertainty) is that the expressions in the main clause are all that L2 learners need to gather a general sense of what is being expressed by the speaker or writer. Nonessential marking of mood on verbs is understood clearly when we compare Romance with a language such as English in which mood is rarely marked. We see no morphological difference between *You speak so rudely to him* and *I hate that you speak so rudely to him*. Similarly, there is no difference in morphology between *He talks too fast* and *I doubt that he talks too fast*. Clearly, English is adequate to express emotion or uncertainty about certain facts or events without morphology marking mood. This only reinforces the idea that subjunctive markers in Romance languages are often unnecessary and redundant in their expression of emotion or uncertainty already communicated lexically.

Pause to consider...

the language that you teach. What are some high-frequency lexical items that communicate tense? Since these expressions appear so often when people are talking about the past, present, or future, can you see how learners would simply skip over verb endings that encode the same meaning? What about expressions of aspect in the language that you teach? Do you think they appear as frequently together with their morphological counterpart (the perfective/imperfective verb ending)?

THE PRIMACY OF MEANING: SOME RESEARCH

VanPatten's principle of meaning before form is evidenced in a number of first language and L2 studies conducted during the mid-1980s (see, for example, Peters, 1985; Sharwood Smith, 1986; and Faerch and Kasper, 1986). VanPatten (2004) posits five subprinciples that pertain to the meaning-before-form processing tendency seen in L2 learners during on-line processing. These subprinciples provide more specifics about what characteristics cause certain items (lexical or morphological in nature) to be overlooked in favor of other items.

The first subprinciple (P1a), called the Primacy of Content Words Principle, is easy to grasp: learners process content words in the input before anything else. This simply means that, with their limited capacity to process the second language, learners display a preference for nouns, verbs, adjectives, and adverbs. They first process these sentential elements that clearly convey the content or overall meaning of an utterance.

*Principle 1.   The Primacy of Meaning Principle. Learners process
input for meaning before they process it for form.*

> **P1a. The Primacy of Content Words Principle.** Learners process content
> words in the input before anything else.
>
> **P1b. The Lexical Preference Principle.** Learners will tend to rely on lexi-
> cal items as opposed to grammatical form to get meaning when both
> encode the same semantic information.
>
> **P1c. The Preference for Nonredundancy Principle.** Learners are more
> likely to process non-redundant meaningful grammatical form
> before they process redundant meaningful forms.
>
> **P1d. The Meaning-before-Nonmeaning Principle.** Learners are more
> likely to process meaningful grammatical forms before nonmeaning-
> ful forms irrespective of redundancy.
>
> **P1e. The Availability of Resources Principle.** For learners to process
> either redundant meaningful grammatical forms or nonmeaningful
> forms, the processing of overall sentential meaning must not drain
> available processing resources.
>
> (VanPatten, 2004)

For example, in the utterance *Marcy went to the store,* the words *Marcy, went,* and
store are more likely to be processed than *to* and *the.* Can you still gather the
meaning of the utterance if you heard only *Marcy went store*? Certainly you can,
and this is the point—L2 learners go for meaning first, and this focus on meaning
drives them to process content words before anything else. L2 learners may
know that larger units of meaning tend to be content words while smaller units
in general tend to be meaningful or nonmeaningful morphological markers. It is
certainly true that even beginning-level learners sometimes process these smaller
units, but they may not be individually analyzed for meaning. That is, they may
be processed along with other larger units of meaning as one whole unanalyzed
"chunk." Prosody can also come into play when learners are attempting to
process an audible input string. Content words typically get more stress and,
within content words themselves, the roots are typically stressed more than the
grammatical affixes that are attached to them. Hence, L2 learners can use
prosody to their advantage as they seek to extract meaning from oral input.

Support for P1a, the Primacy of Content Words Principle, is found in a number of studies involving L2 acquisition of German, Hindi, Spanish, and other languages. For example, in Klein (1986) L2 learners of German performed a sentence
repetition task that required them to repeat utterances that they heard. The results
showed a consistent tendency among learners to repeat the content words (the
"big" words) while words serving a grammatical function were recalled only by
advanced learners. Mangubhai (1991) administered ten weeks of Total Physical
Response (TPR) instruction to five adult L2 learners of Hindi. The results of
Mangubhai's study indicate that all five of his students looked to lexical items for
meaning in the input they received. Finally, in VanPatten (1990), L2 learners of
Spanish who were native speakers of English heard a listening passage in Spanish
on the topic of monetary inflation and then carried out a written recall task in
English. Participants in this study were randomly assigned to four treatment

groups. All four sets of instructions included having them listen to the passage, but three groups received an additional task as well. While group 1 only listened to the passage, group 2 was asked to listen and take written note of all instances of the word *inflación*. Group 3 listened and took note of all instances of the article *la*, while group 4 noted all instances of the third person plural *-n* marker on verbs.

After learners listened to the passage and wrote down anything and everything that they could recall from the passage during the written recall phase, VanPatten tallied the number of correct ideas that learners in each group were able to recall. The results indicated that learners in groups 1 and 2 recalled the same amount of ideas, and groups 3 and 4 recalled significantly fewer ideas than groups 1 and 2. These results lend support to the existence of P1a in that having learners focus on content words presented no hindrance to overall passage comprehension and recall. VanPatten argued that this was due to the fact that learners are engaged in the interpretation of content words first anyway. Therefore, it is only logical that such a task, although formally assigned in this case, would present no extra burden on their attentional resources.

The second subprinciple (P1b), known as the Lexical Preference Principle, states that learners will tend to rely on lexical items as opposed to grammatical form to get meaning when both encode the same semantic information. This means that, for example, when vocabulary and verb endings "compete" to be noticed and processed in an utterance, the vocabulary will more likely win out. We already looked at an example of this when we noted that words like *yesterday* and *tomorrow* are privileged for processing over the verb endings that also communicate past or future, respectively. Another example would be a person/number marker on verbs being overlooked because of explicit subjects that give away who is doing the action. There is no need to process a third person verb ending (*-s* in English) if, for example, the utterance clearly communicates that *Mary* is doing the action. VanPatten (2003) points out that these tendencies in L2 learners to process certain aspects of language before others are not voluntary acts. That is, they are not conscious decisions as some have misunderstood (see DeKeyser, Salaberry, Robinson, and Harrington, 2002).

In a study by Lee, Cadierno, Glass, and VanPatten (1997), Spanish L2 learners were divided into two groups. Both groups received a listening passage; however, the first group's passage included adverbials of time, while the second group's passage did not. The results of the study indicated that participants who received the passage with time-related adverbials performed significantly better than those who did not get the adverbs on a task that required the identification of past, present (progressive), and future events in the passage. This result lends support to P1b in that the learners in this study relied on lexical items (adverbials of time) rather than grammatical form (the verb endings) to determine tense when both encoded the same semantic information. Glass (1994) further extended the study by focusing on the time-of-event identification task using a subset of participants from Lee et al. (1997). Glass replayed from cassette certain portions of the listening passage to the learners and paused to ask them how they decided on past, present, or future for each utterance. A qualitative summary and analysis of learner responses to the inquiries indicated that participants had consistently extracted time-of-event from the lexical cues (adverbs of time) rather than from the verb endings that marked tense.

Other studies also support the existence of P1b. For example, Bardovi-Harlig (1992) found that low-level L2 learners extract time-reference (in this case, past tense) from utterances via lexical markers, and only more advanced learners look to verb morphology for tense. In Musumeci (1989), L2 learners of Italian, French, and Spanish were divided into four treatment groups. Group 1 was asked to interpret individual utterances that included adverbs of time. Group 2 interpreted the same utterances accompanied by hand gestures made by the instructor. Group 3 received both adverbs and hand gestures, while group 4 was given no additional clues and was forced to attend to the verb endings only to determine time of action. The responses of each group showed that the treatment groups that interpreted utterances accompanied by adverbs of time scored significantly higher than did the groups that assigned tense without the aid of lexical cues. As in Lee et al. (1997), Musumeci's results lend support to P1b.

The third subprinciple (P1c), called the Preference for Nonredundancy Principle, states that learners are more likely to process nonredundant meaningful grammatical form before they process redundant meaningful forms. If meaning is already encoded lexically, then learners will not need to process a form. Whereas, if the meaning of a form is not conveyed anywhere else in the utterance, then there is much greater need to process that form. If an utterance contains one redundant form and one nonredundant form, learners are much more likely to notice and subsequently process the latter. For example, in the utterance *Bill likes to go to the movies*, the infinitive *go* is more likely to be processed than the verb ending *-s* on *likes*, because no other sentential element communicates the meaning of *go* (it is nonredundant), whereas we already know that a single individual (*Bill*) is doing the liking. Lee (1987b) is one study that details how L2 learners fail to notice and subsequently process grammatical features that are of lower communicative value during comprehension of written input.

The fourth subprinciple (P1d), the Meaning-Before-Nonmeaning Principle, states that learners are more likely to process meaningful grammatical forms before nonmeaningful forms irrespective of redundancy. For example, in the utterance *La calle oscura estaba llena de peligro* (The dark street was full of danger), the feminine marker *-a* in *oscura* 'dark' and *llena* 'full' is nonmeaningful, whereas the roots of those adjectives and the other content words (*calle, peligro*) carry meaning. P1d then predicts that these meaningful forms are more likely to be processed than is the feminine marker.

Bransdorfer (1989) effectively argued that the preposition *de* (indicating possession) has more communicative value than the definite article *la* 'the.' As in VanPatten (1990), Bransdorfer's subjects were L2 learners of Spanish who were native speakers of English. The participants heard a listening passage in Spanish and then carried out a free recall task in English. All three treatments had learners listen to the passage; however, groups 2 and 3 received an additional task. Group 1 only listened; group 2 listened and took written notes of all instances of the preposition *de;* group 3 listened and noted all instances of the article *la*. A comparison of learner recall scores revealed no statistically significant difference between the performance of groups 1 and 2, and no difference between the performance of groups 2 and 3. However, learners in group 3 recalled significantly fewer ideas than group 1. These results lend support to P1d in that having learners focus on a feature of higher communicative value presented no hindrance to overall passage recall (when compared to group 1), while having them focus on a feature of lower communicative value did bring about a significant effect.

Bransdorfer (1991) replicated his study using *exámenes* 'exams' in place of *de* as the item of higher communicative value and the verb *está* 'is' as the feature of lower communicative value. These items were selected because of the strong stress that both receive in oral input. The results were consistent with Bransdorfer's earlier study in that taking note of the lexical item *exámenes* was not a significant hindrance to passage comprehension. However, noting instances of *está* brought about significantly lower scores on the written recall test.

The fifth subprinciple (P1e), the Availability of Resources Principle, states that for learners to process either redundant meaningful grammatical forms or nonmeaningful forms, the processing of overall sentential meaning must not drain available processing resources. Like the others, this subprinciple presupposes that learners have limitations in their working memory that allow them only to store a finite amount of information during comprehension. Imagine an L2 learner of English is just beginning to notice the present progressive marker *-ing* and hears an utterance such as *Lisa's cousin Jerry, who lives outside of Shreveport, Louisiana, is catching a redeye flight from Houston after she takes a shuttle from Longview.* How likely is it that the learner will process the progressive form in this utterance? Not likely. Why? There is so much to process in this utterance, because of its length and potentially unfamiliar vocabulary. Words like *redeye* and *shuttle* are probably unfamiliar, and the learner's processing resources will most likely be drained.

VanPatten (2004) states that with increased comprehensibility comes the increased likelihood of a form being processed in the input. If the processing of lexical items does not exhaust attentional resources, then the leftover resources can be applied to the processing of redundant or nonmeaningful forms. It might be helpful to think of learners' attentional resources as RAM (random access memory) in a computer. The computer receives lots of data and commands but can carry out only so many operations at one time, depending on the amount of RAM it contains. Similarly, there is so much input that a learner might attend to, but some will most likely get dumped. P1e specifies what tends to get dumped first (redundant forms and nonmeaningful forms) when there is an overload in working memory.

Berne (1992) conducted a replication of VanPatten (1990), this time examining the effects of input simplification on L2 learner comprehension and recall. To effectively simplify the input, Berne first interviewed a group of learners after they had listened to the passage in order to find out which portions of the passage were most difficult and why. Using the information gathered during her interaction with these L2 learners, she simplified the listening passage by shortening the length of some utterances, eliminating complex sentence structures wherever possible and altering the lexical items used if learners reported them as unfamiliar. Berne then administered the simplified passage to a new set of learners divided into four treatment groups. Group 1 only listened to the passage, while group 2 was asked to also take written notes of a content word. Group 3 had to note instances of a verb ending, while group 4 noted instances of an article. After learners listened to the passage, they wrote down all the main ideas that they could recall. When Berne tallied the number of correct

TABLE 2.2 Principle 1(a–e) and Supporting Research

Number	Principle	Research
Principle 1	Primacy of Meaning	Klein (1986); VanPatten (1990); Mangubhai (1991); Bardovi-Harlig (1992); Lee, Cadierno, Glass, & VanPatten (1997); Glass (1994); Musumeci (1989); Bransdorfer (1989); Bransdorfer (1991); Berne (1992); Blau (1990)
P1a	Primacy of Content Words	
P1b	Lexical Preference	
P1c	Preference for Nonredundancy	
P1d	Meaning-Before-Nonmeaning	
P1e	Availability of Resources	

ideas that learners recalled, she found that her results mirrored those of VanPatten (1990) in every way. There was no effect for simplification, or at least no effect that altered the results in such a way that they contrasted with VanPatten's. However, VanPatten (1996) argues that Berne's altered listening passage may not have been simplified enough to bring about results different from those in his 1990 study. Berne's results in isolation are not sufficient to negate any or all effects for input simplification with regard to attentional resources and L2 learners' ability to focus on less or nonmeaningful forms.

Finally, Blau (1990) presented three groups of ESL learners with aural input that was fashioned to be more comprehensible in three unique ways: (1) a decreased rate of speech, (2) simplified sentence structure, and (3) pauses at natural breaks in or between utterances. Blau's results indicate that ESL learners who received input that included pauses comprehended significantly more than those who received the input at a slower rate of speech or in a more simplified state. VanPatten (1996) points out that there may have been some methodological issues concerning Blau's design that call into question the generalizability of her results. Still, Blau's study indirectly suggests that if L2 learners have more time to process input strings (owing to pauses), they may be more likely to notice and subsequently process less or nonmeaningful forms.

The question that we will ask as we examine each of VanPatten's principles throughout the next few chapters is the following: how might an instructor make use of this information in constructing L2 activities for classroom use? There are ways in which instructors can fashion activities that keep in mind the Primacy of Meaning Principle. In order to illustrate just how instructors can take P1 into account, I will examine three grammatical structures—future tense in Italian, past tense in German, and subject-verb agreement in English. I will discuss the processing problem and the activity-design solution for each.

Pause to consider...

the most logical way for instructors to address P1 in their classroom. If the presence of certain lexical cues (*yesterday, tomorrow, John*) give away when the action is taking place or who is doing the action, then what is the most logical solution? Can you guess? Think about it for a moment before moving ahead to the next section.

EXAMPLE 1: FUTURE TENSE IN ITALIAN

As we have already seen, tense is often marked both morphologically and lexically in L2 input. One example among many is the future tense in Italian. Benati (2001) and Benati (2004) are two studies that have looked at the effects of various instruction types on L2 learners' acquisition of the future tense in Italian. Before we take a closer look at those studies, let's examine the processing problem that L2 learners have in noticing future forms in Italian. Consider the following utterances:

(1) *Domani andrò al cinema.*
    Tomorrow I will go to the cinema.
(2) *Ti vedrò più tardi.*
    I will see you later.
(3) *Comincerò il mio corso di ballo la settimana prossima.*
    I will begin my dance class next week.

In each of the three utterances, the reference to a future event is quite clear because of the presence of *domani* 'tomorrow,' *più tardi* 'later,' and *la settimana prossima* 'next week.' This is the processing problem at hand, and there is really only one research-proven solution in terms of instructional intervention—eliminate the adverbials of time in the input and force students to attend to the verb endings themselves to extract meaning with regard to time (tense). This is called *structuring* the input.

The items listed in the *Pause to consider...* box are examples of referential activity items. Referential activity items have only one correct answer and learners must make a decision based on form and meaning. In contrast, affective activity items ask for learners' opinions or beliefs and allow for many possible answers. We will now examine some referential and affective activities for the future tense in Italian.

Pause to consider...

the same utterances that you just read in Italian but without the adverbials of time. Look over the following isolated activity items:

1. *Andrò al cinema...*
   I will go to the cinema...
   a. *ieri*   b. *domani*
      yesterday   tomorrow

2. *Ti vedrò...*
   I will see you...
   a. *più tardi*   b. *la settimana passata*
      later   last week

Referential Activities

In Activity A, students read excerpts from a recent article written about David Beckham, the world's most well-known soccer player. This activity is referential in nature in that there is only one correct answer for each activity item: either the utterance refers to David's present career (with Real Madrid) or it refers to his future plans after his retirement from soccer.

Activity A   David Beckham

In a recent interview, David Beckham was asked about his current life on the road as a professional soccer player and his plans after retirement from soccer. Below are some excerpts from the interview. For each statement, decide whether David is referring to his current life or his plans upon retirement from soccer.

	Now	In Retirement
1. *Conosco gente nuova.* I meet new people.	_____	_____
2. *Viaggerò molto.* I will travel a lot.	_____	_____
3. *Lavorerò sodo.* I will work hard.	_____	_____
4. *Do denaro a organizzazioni di beneficenza.* I give money to charities.	_____	_____
5. *Sarò felice.* I will be happy.	_____	_____
6. *Sarò di buon esempio.* I will be a role model.	_____	_____

[more activity items of the same format]

You should notice a few things about this activity. First, notice that the subject pronoun *io* 'I' has been removed from the activity items. This enables the future (or present) tense verb forms to be the first word in each input string. We briefly looked at P1f (the Sentence Location Principle) in Chapter 1 and we will discuss this at length in the next chapter. For now, simply be aware of the fact that an effort was made to place the targeted form in utterance-initial position for each activity item in order to make it more salient (likely to be processed). Second, notice that there is only one grammatical person and number presented in this activity: first person singular. This adheres to VanPatten's guideline for the design of structured input (SI) activities: *Present one thing at a time.* If a class hour (or a large portion of a class hour) is filled with activities containing the same form, learners will be flooded with exposure to the new form. Having to make decisions about so many examples of the same forms will inevitably lead to form-meaning connections. This is an effective alternative to presenting four, five, or even six forms at once in the same activity. Lastly, you may have noticed that the content words in each utterance do not "give away" the answer. For example, it is logical both that David meets new people now and that he will meet new people in retirement. He certainly travels a lot now to play soccer, but he may also travel a lot for pleasure during his retirement. David probably contributes to some charities at present, but he may also be planning to give during his retirement years. In short, a learner must attend to the verb form itself to arrive at the correct answer. There are no lexical items or subject matters that give away the correct answer. Here, we avoid a very common pitfall in activity design. This and other similar pitfalls will be discussed at length in Chapter 5.

In Activity B we see a combination of referential and affective steps in one SI activity. First, students are asked to read over statements made during a marriage proposal and decide whether each statement refers to current feelings or a promise concerning the future. In this step, there is only one correct answer, and it is based on form and meaning. After completing this referential phase, the students are then asked to answer based on their own opinions. In phase two, the affective portion of this activity, learners must decide whether they believe the statements made. Does Brad Pitt honestly feel this way? Will he really follow through and keep these promises? This is for them to decide based on their own perception of Hollywood stars, celebrity marriages, and these two individuals in particular.

Activity B   Brad Pitt's Marriage Proposal

Marriage is a serious endeavor and it requires commitment from both people. Read over Brad Pitt's statements during his proposal to Jennifer Anniston. For each statement that Brad made, decide whether he was describing his current feelings or whether he was committing to do something for Jennifer in the future. Then, go back and look at each statement and decide whether you believe each statement that Brad made.

	Statement		Believable?	
	Now	Vow	Yes	No
1. *Ti voglio bene.* I care for you.	_____	_____	_____	_____
2. *Sarò sempre fedele.* I will be faithful.	_____	_____	_____	_____
3. *Mi piace stare con te.* I enjoy being with you.	_____	_____	_____	_____
4. *Amerò i tuoi difetti.* I will love your imperfections.	_____	_____	_____	_____
5. *Penso a te.* I think about you.	_____	_____	_____	_____
6. *Soddisfarò tutte le tue necessità.* I will meet all your needs.	_____	_____	_____	_____

Once again, there are no explicit subject pronouns so that the verb forms themselves are encountered first in each utterance. In addition, each statement could theoretically exist in the opposite mode. That is, present tense utterances could have been future promises, and future promises could have been present tense utterances. For example, *I care for you* could have been *I will care for you* and *I will love your imperfections* could have been *I love your imperfections.* In this way, there were no giveaways based on content alone, since learners were forced to attend to the verb forms to answer each item in step one. As with Activity A, Activity B also separates adverbials of time from the utterances and students are asked to connect the time words ("now" or "vow") with each utterance. In this way, the redundancy often seen in raw, unstructured input was avoided, and the Primacy of Meaning Principle was taken into account.

Affective Activities

Now that you have seen an example of a referential activity for the Italian future tense and an example of referential and affective activity items combined into a single two-part activity, let's consider what an exclusively affective activity might look like for the Italian future tense. Activity C departs from the previous activities in that it is not about a celebrity. Instead, this time students must think about their own instructor, his or her habits and routines, and decide whether each of the New Year's resolutions made by the instructor is attainable or not. Obviously, there is no right or wrong answer for these activity items, making it affective in nature. Here, learners simply mark the sentences with a *sì* or a *no* after they assess the probability that their instructor will fulfill each resolution. An activity like this one that is focused on the instructor's daily life is a good way to inject some humor into the classroom and to make the instructor seem more down to earth and approachable.

Like the two previous activities, this affective activity also separates out the adverbial of time and the explicit subject (*L'anno prossimo io...*, in this case) and structures the input in such a way that the future tense verb forms are in utterance initial position. The principal difference between these activities and the referential activities that precede this one is that attending to the verb ending was indispensable for activity completion in the previous activities. Here, with the affective Activity C, it is plausible that someone might grasp the overall meaning of each utterance and respond accordingly (expressing their opinion) without ever noticing or processing the future forms. For this reason, it is more beneficial to learners if referential activities precede affective activities. In this way, affective activity items serve as reinforcement (additional SI) after learners have already begun noticing future forms in the referential activity items.

Activity C   New Year's Resolutions

Your instructor is making New Year's resolutions. Look at the resolutions he/she made for this coming year and indicate whether or not you think your instructor can keep each resolution.

L'anno prossimo io....   *Sì*   *No*

Next year I . . .

1. *arriverò alla lezione in orario.*   _____   _____
   will arrive to class on time.

2. *sarò puntuale nel correggere i compiti.*   _____   _____
   will return homework quickly.

3. *parlerò sempre l'italiano.*   _____   _____
   will always speak in Italian.

4. *non mancherò mai durante le ore d'ufficio.*   _____   _____
   will never miss office hours.

5. *imparerò subito i nomi degli studenti.*   _____   _____
   will learn students' names quickly.

6. *darò il mio numero di telefono di casa.*   _____   _____
   will give out my home phone number.

(Adapted from an activity in Benati, 2001)

Activity D is another affective activity for the Italian future tense. In this activity, the learners themselves become the topic of investigation. Students are asked to read each utterance and decide whether each accurately reflects what they plan to do this coming weekend. Whereas in previous activities, students read excerpts from an article (direct quotes) or statements made by their instructor (again, quotes), here learners are to imagine that these are their own words and then decide whether each is true or false (probable or improbable) for them.

Activity D Your Weekend

What plans do you have for the upcoming weekend? Decide whether each statement is an accurate prediction of what you will do.

		Sì	No
1.	*Studierò molto.* I will study a lot.	_____	_____
2.	*Mi divertirò molto.* I will have a lot of fun.	_____	_____
3.	*Ballerò in un club.* I will dance at a club.	_____	_____
4.	*Visiterò un amico.* I will visit a friend.	_____	_____
5.	*Mangierò in un buon ristorante.* I will eat at a good restaurant.	_____	_____
6.	*Mi riposerò.* I will rest.	_____	_____

All the SI activities for the Italian future tense presented here had certain characteristics in common.

1. They all separated adverbials of time from the future tense verb forms.
2. They all placed the future forms in utterance-initial position.
3. They all focused on just one form (first person singular).

Despite the fact that only the *io* form was used in all these activities, did you notice the variety of topics? Famous people, the instructor, and the students themselves were all utilized as activity themes. With just a little effort to give each activity a context, it is possible to fashion a wide variety of SI activities that all introduce the same grammatical form. This is the flexibility that the *io* form provides in terms of activity themes. In addition, given that the future tense is in focus, one could create a SI activity about the more distant future still using the learners themselves as the topic. This is illustrated in Activity E.

Activity E What Are the Chances?

Step 1. Imagine your life forty years from now. What will it be like? Full of fame and fortune? Or just average? For each statement below, indicate the likelihood of each happening in your life four decades from now.

		Likely	Unlikely
1.	*Avrò molti nipoti.* I will have many grandchildren.	_____	_____

Likely   Unlikely

2.   *Sarò ricco.*
      I will be rich.   _____   _____

3.   *Potrò pensionarmi presto.*
      I will be able to retire early.   _____   _____

4.   *Saprò di più della vita.*
      I will know more about life.   _____   _____

5.   *Farò quello che mi pare e piace.*
      I will do whatever I please.   _____   _____

6.   *Fonderò la mia propria società d'affari.*
      I will start my own company.   _____   _____

Step 2. Now that you have guessed at some of the details in your distant future, give a partner the chance to guess about you as well. Working in pairs, have your partner try to predict which statements you said were "likely" and which ones you said were "unlikely."

Step 3. Now score yourselves on how well you predicted what the other person thinks his or her future will be like. How accurate were you in your predictions? Be ready to share your score with the class.

Activity E also serves to illustrate how follow-up steps can be incorporated into SI activities. Follow-up steps, such as those shown in Step 2 and Step 3, may involve voting, sharing, or comparing answers with a partner, guessing about the truth value of something, reporting your findings to the class, or other similar tasks. These follow-up steps, although not essential, further motivate learners to pay attention to the input, because they know that they will be responsible for the content during a student-student and/or student-teacher interaction that follows. Later in this chapter, you will have the opportunity to revisit some of the activities that we have already seen and design some follow-up steps for them. This will be good practice for you as you begin designing your own SI activities.

Pause to consider...

how each of the activities that you have seen for the Italian future tense took P1 into account. Go back and read through each subprinciple under the Primacy of Meaning Principle and decide whether each was relevant to the design of the activities you have seen so far. How did the activities take into account . . .

- the Primacy of Content Words Principle?
- the Lexical Preference Principle?
- the Availability of Resources Principle?

By now you may have realized that the Primacy of Meaning Principle and its related subprinciples are certainly not limited to affecting future tense structures. Indeed, we see adverbials of time accompanying many past and present constructions as well. To demonstrate how Principle 1 interacts with another verbal structure, we will now take a brief look at past tense in German.

EXAMPLE 2: PAST TENSE IN GERMAN

In the same way that lexical items meaning *tomorrow* and *next year* might prevent learners from processing future forms in Italian, words like *yesterday* and *last year* communicate past tense and may leave past tense verb markers undetected in the input. To combat the tendency that L2 learners have to rely on lexical cues as a time indicator, once again all adverbials of time in the following activities for German have been either removed or separated from the utterances containing the past tense forms. In addition, German has a verb-must-come-second rule, but in the following activities the subjects have been removed to make past forms more salient. Again, we will discuss the Sentence Location Principle at length in Chapter 3.

What sets Activity F apart from the others that you have seen thus far in this chapter is that it requires the instructor to read from a script. This gives the learners an opportunity to listen to the novel forms in the input. Having the chance to make sound-meaning connections is just as important, if not more important, than making written form-meaning connections. Since the focus of any communicative approach to language instruction is on interactive exchange and much of this exchange occurs orally, it is crucial that learners be given contextualized interpretation practice in the aural mode. In this activity, students listen to various statements about Hillary Clinton and then make a decision about each statement based on form and meaning. The past tense verb form is the first thing that learners hear; the subject "Hillary" has been purposefully removed from each utterance to allow for this. In addition, you will notice that there are no time referents or lexical giveaways ("White House," and so on) in the activity items. By eliminating all other cues except for the past tense morphology, L2 learners of German must notice and process the meaning of each present or past tense form in order to complete the activity successfully.

Activity F   Hillary Rodham Clinton—First Lady and Senator

Listen to each statement made about the life of Hillary Clinton and decide whether it is referring to her past life as First Lady or her present life as a New York senator.

As First Lady   As Senator

1. _____   _____

2. _____   _____

3. _____   _____

4. _____   _____

5. _____   _____

6. _____   _____

INSTRUCTOR'S SCRIPT

war bei wichtigen Sitzungen anwesend.
attended important meetings.

trifft viele Weltführer.
meets many world leaders.

ist oft im Fernsehen.
appears often on TV.

reservierte Zeit für die Familie.
reserved time for family.

las vertrauliche Dokumente.
read confidential documents.

spricht mit Beredsamkeit.
speaks with eloquence.

Once again, a nice alternative to a Hollywood celebrity, sports figure, or politician is someone whom the learner knows well such as an immediate family member, a relative, a best friend, or the instructor. In this next activity, learners have to imagine what the teen years were like for one of their parents, another relative, and their instructor. In the last *Pause to consider . . .* box you were asked to look over both of these activities and decide which one is affective in nature and which one is referential. If you thought that Activity G was affective, you answered correctly. (Activity F is indeed referential.) In Activity G, there is no right or wrong answer based on the utterances learners read; instead, they are merely hypothesizing about what might be true. Only through a follow-up with these individuals could students verify whether their answers to each activity item were correct or not. In fact, this would be a great follow-up step to do with the Instructor column. If learners know that they will actually learn of the truth about their instructor concerning each of the activity items, they may be more motivated to try to guess correctly. In many classroom settings, making an SI activity into a competition or game works very well to motivate student attention to the input and participation in general.

Activity G   In their teens . . .

Imagine what one of your parent's life was like as a teenager many years ago. What about another relative? Your instructor? Can you imagine who fancied himself or herself as a romantic? A reckless partyer? Read over each of the statements and decide whether each individual (parent, relative, instructor) likely did these things or not.

He/She . . .	Parent	Relative	Instructor
1. *fuhr ohne Führerschein.* drove without a license.	———	———	———
2. *trank minderjährig.* drank while underage.	———	———	———
3. *hatte viele Freunde/Freundinnen.* had many boyfriends/girlfriends.	———	———	———
4. *fiel eine oder mehr Prüfungen durch.* failed one or more tests.	———	———	———
5. *stritt mit einem Lehrer.* quarreled with a teacher.	———	———	———
6. *schrieb Gedichte.* wrote poems.	———	———	———

After seeing some SI activities for both future tense and past tense, you have probably thought about whether the Primacy of Meaning Principle can affect how learners process grammatical structures that are not related to tense. Earlier in this chapter, you may have looked over Table 2.1 containing some structures in a number of languages that can potentially interact with learners' tendency to process meaning before form, and lexical items before morphological markers, when they both encode the same meaning. We will now take a brief look at one more of these grammatical forms and examine how SI can promote noticing a form that might otherwise go undetected by beginning-level learners of English.

Pause to consider...

the characteristics that these last two activities for past tense in German have in common with the previous activities for the future tense in Italian. Did you notice the consistency in . . .

- removing all adverbials of time from the activity items?
- presenting the novel verb forms in utterance-initial position?
- having learners *do something* with the input?

EXAMPLE 3: SUBJECT-VERB AGREEMENT IN ENGLISH

You would think that the third person singular *-s* marker for present tense verbs in English would be quite easy for L2 learners of English to acquire. After all, there are only two forms for most present tense verbs in English. (The verb *to be* is an exception, with three forms: *am, is,* and *are.*) For instance, with the verb *to walk,* we can generate the following paradigm:

	Singular		Plural	
1st person	I	walk	We	walk
2nd person	You	walk	You	walk
3rd person	He/She	walks	They	walk

Note that a learner needs to acquire only two forms, *walk* and *walks.* Despite the fact that there are only two forms to learn, beginning and even intermediate ESL learners often do not notice or process the third person singular marker *-s* in the input. Why not? The reason is that in all naturally occurring contexts, it is not necessary to process the *-s* marker in order to comprehend the meaning of the utterance. Since English mandates the presence of an explicit subject, there is seldom a doubt as to who is doing the action or to whom the verb is referring.

You will recall that with the SI activities for tense (Italian future and German past), it was necessary to structure the input so that the adverbials of time were removed entirely or separated from the input containing the verbal morphology. This was an effort to keep the learners' processing strategies in mind, taking into account the fact that learners' primary goal is to extract meaning (before form) and that they do this by first looking to content words. Similarly, it will be necessary with the present tense marker *-s* in English to make sure that learners cannot rely on a lexical item (here, explicit subjects) to process the overall meaning of the activity items. Activity H is an example of how this might be done.

Activity H   Pop Culture Icons

A recent article in a pop culture magazine summarized the lives and contributions of major figures in the rock'n'roll industry. Below are just a few excerpts from the article. For each excerpt, decide whether the author of the article was referring to Sarah McLachlan or to both Bono and the Edge.

	Sarah McLachlan	Bono and the Edge
1 .... travels all over the world.	———	———
2 .... play the guitar.	———	———
3 .... sings before thousands.	———	———
4 .... writes a lot of songs.	———	———
5 .... make videos for MTV and VH1.	———	———
6 .... raises money for charities.	———	———

Just as lexical items communicating tense were removed in previous activities, now the subjects ("Sarah McLachlan" and "Bono and the Edge") have been separated from each of the six activity items. In fact, the objective of this activity is precisely to find out to whom each utterance refers. Is this an affective activity, or is it referential in nature? Remember the question to ask is this: is there only one correct answer to each item? Indeed, there is only one right response to each activity item in Activity H, making it a referential activity. It may be true that Sarah McLachlan, Bono, and the Edge all play the guitar and sing before thousands, but based on the forms used in each utterance they can refer only to one musician or a group of musicians but not both. In fact, I purposely eliminated the possibility of arriving at the correct answer based on content alone. For each activity item, if one were to exclude the verb form, the content of the utterances are plausible for either Sarah or Bono and the Edge. In this way, there are no giveaways; rather, there is only purposed ambiguity until one processes the verb form itself.

Now you have seen how Principle 1 interacts with both tense and subject-verb agreement. Before we conclude this chapter by looking at some research on SI that relates to Principle 1, I have included one final sample activity, which is an affective activity that might follow Activity H for introducing the third person singular marker *-s*. In Activity I, the instructor cannot predict how learners will respond to each activity item, and there is certainly more than one plausible answer because responses are based on student opinion.

Activity I   Lifestyles of the Irresponsible and Studious

What is it like living with your roommate? Did you hit the jackpot or come up with the short straw? For the routines and habits described below, indicate how often your roommate does each. (Choose only one roommate; if you live alone then you can respond based on your best friend's lifestyle.)

My roommate . . .

	Never	Sometimes	Frequently
1 . . . . stays up past 1 A.M.	_____	_____	_____
2 . . . . parties during the week.	_____	_____	_____
3 . . . . skips classes.	_____	_____	_____
4 . . . . studies a lot.	_____	_____	_____
5 . . . . cheats on exams.	_____	_____	_____

Here, learners fill out a survey about their roommate's routine and habits. One can imagine how responding to such a survey can lead to humorous comments and an interesting follow-up discussion. However, this activity can be effective not only because of its content but also because of its structure. Again, we see that the form to be processed is encountered in utterance-initial position (thus, taking into account the Sentence Location Principle), and the subject "My roommate" has been extracted from the input strings in order to push learners to attend to the target forms.

Thus far in this chapter you have been exposed to a number of examples of SI activities that take into account the Primacy of Meaning Principle and its corresponding subprinciples. Now, it is your turn to begin the process of activity design.

PRINCIPLES IN PRACTICE

In this Principles in Practice section, you will work through three different tasks that will prepare you for the design of your own SI activities for Principle 1.

TASK A. If you go back and look at activities A–E of this chapter, you will notice that, for each activity, there are only six items given as examples. See if you can add two more activity items to complete each activity. Be ready to share your activity items with your colleagues. (Of course, you may write your items in English or Italian, depending on the makeup of the group to whom you will present.)

TASK B. Of all of the activities in this chapter, only Activity E included follow-up steps. Go back and look over the follow-up steps (Steps 2 and 3) in Activity E and then design your own follow-up steps for three of the other activities in this chapter: one for an Italian activity (A, B, C, or D), one for a German activity (F or G), and one for an ESL activity (H or I).

TASK C. Select a grammatical structure from the language that you teach and design two SI activities—one referential activity and one affective activity. One of the activities should require listening to input and making decisions about the aural stimuli. You may want to review the difference between referential and affective activities before you begin working. Also, remember to adhere to these four guidelines from VanPatten (1996) that were discussed in Chapter 1 as you create your activities.

1. Present one thing (one function or use) at a time.
2. Keep meaning in focus.
3. Have learners do something with the input.
4. Keep the learners' processing strategies (in this case, Principle 1) in mind.

THREE SAMPLE STUDIES

Cadierno (1995) investigated the effects of processing instruction (SI + hints for processing) on the acquisition of the preterite tense in Spanish. Because learners may use adverbs to assign tense to an utterance, Cadierno eliminated all adverbs of time from her SI activities so that learners were forced to attend to the verb endings to assign tense. Participants were divided into three groups: a traditional production-focused group, a processing instruction group, and a control group. The results of her study revealed that learners who received processing instruction performed better than the other two groups on both comprehension and production tests, even though the processing instruction group was never asked to produce any preterite forms during the treatment.

In Benati (2001), participants enrolled in a second-semester Italian course were assigned to one of two treatments: processing instruction (PI) and traditional output-based instruction. The processing instruction treatment consisted of SI activities that were similar to Activities A–E in this chapter and some explicit information (EI) about the Italian future tense and the Principle 1–related hindrances that may affect the noticing and processing of future forms in Italian. The output group received a traditional grammar explanation and production-oriented activities. Note that the PI group *never produced* a single future tense verb form at any time during the instructional period. They only interpreted the SI containing preformed future forms in Italian. The traditional output group only produced the future forms and was never asked to interpret any SI. The purpose of Benati's study was to investigate whether or not PI and/or output-based instruction would bring about improved performance on tasks involving the interpretation and production of future forms in Italian and whether the improvement would be statistically similar for both instruction types. The results of Benati (2001) are provided in Table 2.3.

Benati found that PI (SI + EI) had an overall greater effect than the output-focused treatment group. The group that received SI improved significantly more than the other group on the interpretation task and produced future forms just as well. The results of this study are consistent with other PI research, and they highlight the indispensable role that input plays in second

TABLE 2.3 Mean Score on Interpretation and Production Tasks for the PI and Output Groups in Benati (2001)

	Processing Instruction (*n* = 13)	Output-Based Instruction (*n* = 13)
Interpretation Task		
Pretest	3.6	3.8
Immediate Post-Test	8.2	5.8
Post-Test 2	8.0	5.6
Production Task		
Pretest	2.5	2.4
Immediate Post-Test	7.3	7.6
Post-Test 2	6.8	7.5

language acquisition (SLA) and the benefits of SI in particular. You can read more about Benati's study in the May 2001 issue of *Language Teaching Research.*

Benati (2004) investigated whether SI activities + EI would bring about greater improvement than SI alone on tasks involving the interpretation and production of the Italian future tense. For this study, Benati used second semester learners of Italian whose native language was English. The instruction took place over two consecutive days and there were three treatment groups: those who received only EI, those who received only SI activities, and those who received both EI and SI activities. This last group was referred to as the Processing Instruction or PI group. Raw scores were calculated for an aural interpretation task and a written production task with the maximum score being 10 for each task. The interpretation task contained ten target items worth one point each, and the production task contained five items worth two points each. (Learners received one point on the production task if a form's ending was correct but the root was somehow misspelled.) Benati found no difference between the PI (EI + SI) group and the SI-only group on the interpretation task, and both groups improved significantly more than the group that received only EI. The gains made by the PI and SI groups held through a second post-test conducted a

TABLE 2.4 Mean Score and Standard Deviation on Interpretation and Production Tasks for the PI (*n* = 14), SI (n = 12) and EI (n = 12) Groups in Benati (2004)

	Processing Instruction		Structured Input		Explicit Information	
	Mean	SD	Mean	SD	Mean	SD
Interpretation Task						
Pretest	2.70	.91	2.10	.94	2.60	1.07
Immediate Post-Test	8.30	1.00	7.80	1.27	4.60	2.02
Post-Test 2	7.70	1.19	7.50	1.38	3.80	1.28
Production Task						
Pretest	2.20	.80	1.90	.90	1.80	.83
Immediate Post-Test	7.30	1.34	6.50	1.47	3.10	.91
Post-Test 2	6.50	.94	4.80	.92	2.50	.97

month later. PI and SI also brought about equally improved performance on the written production task, and both groups again outperformed the group that received EI only. A summary of the descriptive statistics for Benati (2004) is provided in Table 2.4.

You can read more about this study of the effects of EI on learners who receive SI activities in Chapter 12 of Benati's *Processing Instruction* (Erlbaum Press, 2004).

READ MORE ABOUT IT

Benati, A. (2001). A comparative study of the effects of processing instruction and output-based instruction on the acquisition of the Italian future tense. *Language Teaching Research, 5,* 95–127.

Benati, A. (2004). The effects of structured input activities and explicit information on the acquisition of the italian future tense. In VanPatten, B. (ed.), *Processing instruction: Theory, research, and commentary.* Mahwah, NJ: Erlbaum.

Cadierno, T. (1995). Formal instruction from a processing perspective: An investigation into the Spanish past tense. *Modern Language Journal 79,* 179–193.

CHAPTER 3

The Sentence
Location Principle

INTRODUCTION

Take about ten seconds to read the following numbers:

16   71   84   56   67   49   32   75   93   28

Now, without looking, write down all of the numbers that you remember from the list. If you are like most people, you more easily recalled the numbers 16 and 28, whereas you could not remember some of the numbers near the middle of the list. If you were to conduct this type of experiment with a large group, you would find highly consistent results that inform us about how humans function as information processors. We have already seen that L2 learners' working memory has a limited capacity for processing. This limitation implies that learners are forced to privilege certain aspects of language over others during on-line processing. Concerning the limitations of learners' working memory, VanPatten (2003) states the following:

> I take as a point of departure the following claims: that during interaction in the L2 (1) learners are focused primarily on the extraction of meaning from the input (e.g., Faerch and Kasper, 1986; Krashen, 1982), (2) **that learners must somehow "notice" things in the input for acquisition to happen** (Schmidt, 1990 and elsewhere), and that (3) **noticing is constrained by working memory limitations regarding the amount of information they can hold and process** during on-line (or real-time) computation of sentences during comprehension (e.g., Just and Carpenter, 1993).

Just as you were probably not able to hold in memory all ten numbers listed above, L2 learners are not always able to notice and process all the forms within a given utterance. In this chapter, we look at VanPatten's (2004) P1f, a principle that helps explain why forms in the middle of an utterance may not be noticed or processed by L2 learners.

The Sentence Location Principle implies that learners are sensitive to position within an utterance. The easiest forms to process are those located in initial position within an utterance. The second easiest forms to process occur in utterance-final position. The most difficult forms to process are those that occur in the middle parts of utterances. Before we begin activity design, as we have done in the previous chapter, we look at some structures affected by P1f and some of the research related to learner sensitivity to position within an utterance.

Principle 1f

P1f. Learners tend to process items in sentence-initial position before those in final position and those in medial position.

GRAMMATICAL FORMS AFFECTED BY P1f

What grammatical forms might be affected by P1f? Table 3.1 lists some of the principal grammatical features from five different languages that are *often* found in sentence-medial position. For this reason, they may be difficult features for an L2 learner to notice and subsequently process.

Note that this principle is quite different from some of the other principles introduced in Chapter 1. For example, you read that the First Noun Principle causes learners to assign the role of subject to the first noun or pronoun they encounter. Therefore, when a direct object pronoun is the first element in an utterance, learners may assume that it is the subject. Even though learners misinterpret the DO pronoun, they do *notice* it. In contrast, due to P1f, learners may *not even notice* a particular form that is located in utterance-medial position, much less process it.

As you can see, some fundamental grammatical forms in a variety of languages interact with P1f and therefore may go undetected by the L2 learner. In fact, some of the forms listed in Table 3.1 are not acquired until very late. P1f suggests that the delay may be due to their frequent appearance in the middle of the sentence, rather than in the initial or final utterance position. However, many of these forms *do not always* appear in utterance-medial position. That is, there are contexts in which some of the features listed are found in sentence-ini-

TABLE 3.1 Examples of Grammatical Forms Affected by P1f

Spanish	French	Italian	English (ESL)	German
Subjunctive mood	Subjunctive mood	Subjunctive mood	3rd singular -*s* marker	Case markers
Object pronouns	Object pronouns	Object pronouns	Object pronouns	Object pronouns
Tense markers	Tense markers	Tense markers	Tense markers	Tense markers
Aspectual markers	Aspectual markers	Aspectual markers	Aspectual markers	Aspectual markers
Certain prepositions	Certain prepositions	Certain prepositions	Certain prepositions	
	Negation with *Avoir*	Adjective Agreement		

tial and/or sentence-final position as well. In addition, note that P1f may not be the *only* factor making these features difficult to notice and subsequently process. Often, as we will see in our two examples ahead, there is more than one principle interacting with a given language feature.

Pause to consider...

the language that you teach. Which of the forms listed in Table 3.1 can also appear in initial position? How often? Which can appear in final position? What other forms in the language that you teach are found in ...

1. utterance-initial position?
2. utterance-medial position?
3. utterance-final position?

THE SENTENCE LOCATION PRINCIPLE: SOME RESEARCH

We have just introduced the idea that learners are able to process utterance-initial items more easily than they process items in sentence-final position and that utterance-medial forms are the most difficult to process. Neisser (1967) investigated *mnemonics* and concluded that memorization of a string of elements is subject to both *primacy effects* and *recency effects,* resulting in better memorization of initial and final elements. Two decades later, research on first language acquisition (e.g., Peters, 1985) suggested that children are predisposed to process sentence-initial and sentence-final positions more easily than other positions. Barcroft and VanPatten point out that learner sensitivity to position within an utterance has been evidenced in L2 learning as well. For example, Klein (1986) looked at native speakers of Italian and Spanish who were asked to reproduce a series of German utterances that they had just heard. Overall, performance on the repetition task varied between subjects and between utterances. However, all learners consistently remembered the first and last words of the utterances. Klein's results support the idea that initial and final segments of an utterance are privileged for analysis more readily than are other portions of an utterance. Barcroft and VanPatten found similar results in that sentence initial elements were processed more easily than were other elements. However, their results differed from Klein's in that utterance-final elements were not privileged over elements in medial position. Rosa and O'Neill (1998) replicated a portion of the Barcroft and VanPatten design, and the results practically mirrored those of the original study. However, Rosa and O'Neill did find that, for three of the four target items tested, learners showed a preference for stimulus-final words over stimulus-medial words. Other studies related to utterance position (for example, see Kim, 1995) have produced only slightly different results from these.

With this principle in mind, the obvious question is this: how might an instructor make use of this information in constructing SI activities? As we have

---

DEFINITIONS

Mnemonics: From the Greek word *mnemon* (mindful). Mnemonics are ways or devices (mental pictures, stories, and so on) used for remembering a list of unrelated items in a particular order.

Primacy Effect: When an item within a string is remembered more easily because it is encountered (heard or read) first in a string of items.

Recency Effect: When an item within a string is remembered more easily because it is encountered last.

seen with Principle 1 in the last chapter, there are ways for instructors to manipulate input so that medial-position items do not fall to the wayside. Now we will take a closer look at two grammatical structures that are affected by P1f in order to discuss how to design good SI activities for them.

EXAMPLE 1: THE SPANISH SUBJUNCTIVE

To understand how this principle affects the processing of a grammatical form, we will take the Spanish subjunctive mood as a point of departure. Present tense subjunctive forms are generally formed (with some exceptions) by using the present tense *yo* (first person singular) root and adding an "opposite" ending—an *a* ending for verbs that usually take *e,* or an *e* ending for verbs that usually take *a.* For example, the indicative *habla* (speaks; third person singular) becomes *hable,* and the indicative *come* (eats; third person singular) becomes *coma.* Subjunctive forms are generally located in subordinate clauses introduced by *que* 'that.' For the purpose of the following illustration, we limit our discussion to one use of the subjunctive: that is, when a speaker communicates uncertainty about something. Below are just a few examples of when the subjunctive might be used following an opinion phrase of uncertainty:

(1) *Dudo que Ana hable bien el ruso.*
I doubt that Ana speaks (*subj.*) Russian well.
(2) *Es posible que llueva.*
It's possible that it will rain (*subj*).
(3) *No creo que gane Woods otra vez.*
I don't think that Woods will win (*subj.*) again.

It is common knowledge among Spanish language teachers that learners do not acquire the subjunctive mood until extremely late, if at all. Some research over the last decade suggests that the subjunctive should be taught only to advanced learners of Spanish. Joseph Collentine, who is known for his work with the Spanish subjunctive, concluded that the time devoted to teaching the subjunctive mood at beginning levels should be reduced, because beginners are not ready to acquire mood (Collentine, 1993). In addition, Pereira (1996) compared a group of third-semester learners that received instruction on subjunctive forms with a control group that received no instruction. She found only a very small effect for instruction, and her results lend support to Collentine's claim. Collentine (1995) went on to suggest that instruction on mood selection in Spanish may not even be very beneficial to intermediate-level learners, because they still lack the ability to process complex sentence structures.

In a majority of Spanish utterances that include a subjunctive form, the subjunctive is located in sentence-medial position—where it is least likely to be noticed and processed. For this reason, the Spanish subjunctive is a good example of the effects of P1f on processing. For example, in the utterance *Dudo que Ana hable bien el ruso* (I doubt that Ana speaks Russian well), the subjunctive form *hable* 'speaks' is found in the middle of the sentence. P1f predicts that learners will tend to gloss over (not noticing and not processing) the subjunctive ending *-e,* because it is not in one of the more salient positions (sentence initial or sentence final).

Also, note that P1 (discussed in Chapter 2) is relevant to the Spanish subjunctive, and, therefore, P1 will affect the design of the sample activities presented in the next section as well. P1(a) and (b) imply that lexical form is weighted more heavily than grammatical form in its importance to the learner's input processor. In sentences like *Dudo que Ana hable bien el ruso*, the nonaffirmative phrase *Dudo* 'I doubt' communicates uncertainty to the learner. There is no reason for the learner to attend to the subjunctive verb ending (*-e* in *hable*), because it simply marks the uncertainty *already* expressed. That is, *Dudo* and the *-e* ending encode the same meaning. Once a learner has processed *Dudo* for meaning, the *-e* ending in *hable* provides no new information and may go unprocessed.

We will now look at some sample SI activities for the Spanish subjunctive. Before reading on, consider what activities might look like that place subjunctive forms in utterance-initial position to make them more salient.

Pause to consider...

how you might actually make use of P1f with the Spanish subjunctive. Note how not having to reread the phrase *No creo que...* (I don't think that . . .) makes the subjunctives that follow a little easier to notice.

1. *No creo que cante bien.*   I don't think that he/she sings well.
2. *No creo que baile el tango.*   I don't think that he/she dances the tango.
3. *No creo que salga pronto.*   I don't think that he/she leaves soon.
4. *No creo que diga la verdad.*   I don't think that he/she tells the truth.

Because *No creo que...* is repeated, noticing the forms in the last portion of each utterance is fairly easy now, isn't it? What else could we do to make noticing subjunctives easier? Is it possible to design an activity that places subjunctive forms in utterance-initial position?

Referential Activities

Before we begin looking at sample SI activities for P1f, recall from Chapters 1 and 2 that there are two main types of SI activities: referential and affective. Do you remember what these terms mean? Which type of activity items . . .

     1. . . . asks for an opinion?
     2. . . . has only one correct answer?

If you remembered correctly, referential activities require the learner to focus on form and, for each item, to make a decision about meaning based on form. Hence, referential activity items allow for only one correct answer. In contrast, affective activities allow for numerous possible answers based on one's opinions, beliefs, or feelings.

Because the subjunctive is a redundant feature in Spanish, referential activities for the Spanish subjunctive should be structured such that the learner is required to choose the *correct* main clause—either one of certainty or one of doubt—based on whether or not the verb that follows has an indicative ending or a subjunctive ending. As illustrated in Activity A, the subjunctive forms are no longer embedded in each activity item. Rather, learners read or listen to the last portion of an utterance beginning with the subjunctive form. Notice how the main clause is separated out and that utterance-medial forms become utterance-initial forms. That is, the subjunctives that were embedded are now at the beginning of each activity item. Learners read the subordinate clauses and then select an opinion phrase to correctly begin each sentence.

Activity A is a written, referential activity. Learners read the subordinate clause (the end of the sentence) and have to select the main clause (the beginning of the sentence) that fits. Through an activity of this structure, we achieve two main objectives.

1. The subjunctive forms are no longer in utterance-medial position.
2. The uncertainty phrases no longer take precedence for processing over the subjunctive verb endings.

Activity A   Shaquille O'Neal

The Miami Heat's Shaquille O'Neal has won several NBA championship rings. Below are a reporter's comments about Shaq. For each statement, decide if the reporter believes it or doubts it. Circle the opinion phrase that correctly begins each comment.

1. ... *sea un hombre perezoso.*   ... is a lazy man.
   a. Creo que   a. I believe that (he)
   b. Es dudoso que   b. It is doubtful that (he)

2. ... *es el mejor jugador del mundo.*   ... is the best player in the world.
   a. Estoy seguro   a. I am sure (he)
   b. Dudo que   b. I doubt that (he)

3. ... *come en Burger King con frecuencia.*   ... eats at Burger King frequently.
   a. Es cierto que   a. It is certain that (he)
   b. Es posible que   b. It is possible that (he)

4. ... *lea muchas novelas en su tiempo libre.*   ... reads many novels in his free time.
   a. Todos saben que   a. Everyone knows that (he)
   b. Todos dudan que   b. Everyone doubts that (he)

5. ... *le guste hablar con los reporteros.*   ... likes to talk with reporters.
   a. Es cierto que   a. It is certain that (he)
   b. No es verdad que   b. It isn't true that (he)

6. ... *siempre lleva ropa elegante.*   ... always wears elegant clothes.
   a. *Es evidente que*   a. It is evident that (he)
   b. *No es evidente que*   b. It is not evident that (he)

[more activity items of the same format]

For Activity B, learners will *hear* the subordinate clause, and they must then select the main clause that best completes each sentence. Recall from Chapter 1 that it is important to give students the opportunity to interpret *aural* input as well as written input. In Activity B, the instructor reads the script, and students have to attend to the forms they hear in order to answer each item. Notice that the activity does not ask students for their own opinion (as an affective activity might), but rather it requires them to make decisions about utterances based on making a form-meaning connection.

Activity B   Your Instructor

You will hear the second half of a statement that someone recently made about your instructor. Circle the opinion phrase that correctly fits with each statement.

			INSTRUCTOR'S SCRIPT
1.	*Yo sé que...*	I know that . . .	1. *coma en casa mucho.* eats at home a lot.
	No creo que...	I don't believe that . . .	
2.	*Es obvio que...*	It is obvious that . . .	2. *baile mucho en las discotecas.* goes dancing a lot in the clubs
	Dudo que...	I doubt that . . .	
3.	*Es evidente que...*	It is evident that . . .	3. *es muy inteligente.* is very intelligent.
	No es cierto que...	It is not certain that . . .	
4.	*Es cierto que...*	It is certain that . . .	4. *haga mucho ejercicio.* exercises much.
	No pienso que...	I don't think that . . .	
5.	*Es verdad que...*	It's true that . . .	5. *come comida rápida todos los días.* eats fast food every day.
	Es posible que...	It's possible that . . .	
6.	*Creo que...*	I believe that . . .	6. *sea un poco perezoso.* is a little lazy.
	No opino que...	I don't suppose that . . .	
7.	*Es obvio que...*	It is obvious that . . .	7. *tenga menos de 23 años.* is less than 23 years old.
	Es imposible que...	It is impossible that . . .	

[Note: the subject (he or she) is understood in each item above]

Activity B demonstrates how an oral SI activity might look. In Activity C, we see a slightly different format for a written referential activity. Note that there are only two opinion phrases (total) for the entire activity. This alternative structure may serve to highlight the contrast between indicatives and subjunctives (i.e., between certainty and uncertainty) more easily for the learner.

Activity C   Ben Affleck

The phrases below come from a magazine article about Ben Affleck. Indicate whether the author believes each idea or doubts each idea. Place an X under the opinion that fits with each phrase.

Creo que...   *Dudo que...*

I believe that . . .   I doubt that . . .

_____   _____   **1.** *sea un buen actor.*
                                (he) is a good actor.

_____   _____   **2.** *gana mucho dinero.*
                                (he) earns a lot of money.

_____   _____   **3.** *tiene una casa muy grande.*
                                (he) has a very big house.

_____   _____   **4.** *tenga una novia.*
                                (he) has a girlfriend.

_____   _____   **5.** *cante muy bien.*
                                (he) sings very well.

_____   _____   **6.** *está contento con su carrera.*
                                (he) is happy with his career.

_____   _____   **7.** *es guapo.*
                                (he) is handsome.

_____   _____   **8.** *le guste la publicidad.*
                                (he) is pleased by the publicity.

Affective Activities

In contrast to referential activities, recall that affective activities have more than one correct answer. Learners are no longer being forced to make form-meaning connections; rather, they are now given a context in which to offer their own opinions or beliefs. They may also offer responses based on their knowledge of the world around them. In the referential activities illustrated in the previous section, learners selected which matrix clause correctly completed each utterance. In the affective SI activities that follow, both the matrix clauses and the subordinate clauses are already provided.

Activity D   Regis's House

You probably know a little about the success of Regis Philbin, former host of the television show "Who Wants to Be a Millionaire?" Below are some statements about his home and his home life. Place a check next to the statements that seem logical to you.

1. *Es probable que su casa...*   It is probable that his house . . .

_____ *tenga aire acondicionado.*   has air conditioning.

_____ *esté en un barrio seguro.*   is in a secure neighborhood.

_____ *sea muy pequeña.*   is very small.

2. *Dudo que su casa...*   I doubt that his house . . .

_____ *sea semejante a mi casa.*   is similar to my house.

_____ *tenga solamente un piso.*   has only one floor.

3. *No creo que Regis...*   I don't believe that Regis . . .

_____ *tenga animales domésticos.*   has pets.

_____ *limpie su propia casa.*   cleans his own house.

[more activity items of the same format]

It is also possible to design an affective activity around only *one* opinion phrase, as seen in Activity E about the *National Enquirer*. Here, students are working only with the phrase *No creo que...* (I don't believe that . . .). Due to its clear and simple format, this activity might precede other affective activities that involve more than one opinion phrase.

Activity E   The Enquirer

Below are some opinions about the newspaper *The National Enquirer*. Check off the opinions with which you agree.

No creo que la Enquirer...   I don't believe that the *Enquirer* . . .

_____ *haga buenas investigaciones.*   does good investigations.

_____ *diga la verdad en los artículos.*   tells the truth in its articles.

_____ *sea conocida en otros países.*   is recognized in other countries.

_____ *pague mucho dinero por la información.*   pays a lot of money for information.

_____ *se publique en español.*   is published in Spanish.

_____ *sea de interés en esta clase.*   is of interest in this class.

Note that in all the referential and affective activities presented so far, the main clause was separated from the subordinate clause. This was a deliberate attempt to take advantage of the fact that the first element in a sentence is processed more easily than a sentence-medial element. The once medially occurring subjunctives are now in a privileged processing position.

Pause to consider...

Activity F, then answer the following questions.

1. **Would learners need to attend to the subjunctive forms as in other activities you have seen? Why or why not?**
2. **How might you restructure this activity to make it more effective?**

Activity F   Predicting the Future

Below are some predictions about the future. Indicate whether you agree or disagree with each opinion. Would you ever be caught saying these things?

¿Estás de acuerdo? (Do you agree?)

Sí	No	
_____	_____	**1.** *Es probable que haya otra guerra mundial.* It is likely that there will be another world war.
_____	_____	**2.** *Es imposible que una mujer sea presidente de los EEUU.* It's impossible that a woman will be president of the U.S.
_____	_____	**3.** *Es probable que el mundo se termine pronto.* It is likely that the world will end soon.
_____	_____	**4.** *No creo que las computadoras vayan a controlar el mundo.* I don't believe that computers will control the world.
_____	_____	**5.** *Es posible que haya vida en otros planetas.* It's possible that there is life on other planets.

[more activity items of the same format]

EXAMPLE 2: THE FRENCH AVOIR + NEGATION

Another good example of a grammatical structure that interacts with P1f has to do with the French infinitive *avoir* 'to have' and negation. When a French speaker uses the verb *avoir* with the negative marker *ne/n'... pas* surrounding the verb (to express " . . . do/does *not* have . . ."), the indefinite article that follows—*un, une,* or *des*—must be changed to *de* (or *d'* if preceding a vowel). For example, *Philippe a une maison à Paris* (Philippe has a house in Paris) becomes

*Philippe n'a pas **de** maison à Paris* (Philippe does not have a house in Paris). Similarly, *Françoise a un oiseau jaune* (Francoise has a yellow bird) becomes *Françoise n'a pas **d'**oiseau jaune* (Francoise does not have a yellow bird).

Because the *de* marker is typically found in utterance-medial position, this marker is not likely to be processed by the L2 learner of French. Once again, by structuring activity items with the *de* marker in a more salient position, learners are more likely to detect the marker and to process the distinction between *un(e)* and *de*. That is, they would be more likely to connect *un(e)* with affirmative statements and *de/d'* with negative statements. In addition, just as with the Spanish subjunctive, note that P1 may be at work with this grammatical feature as well. The *de/d'* marker is a redundant feature that simply marks the negation a second time. In the examples given above, one can see that negation is already expressed by the words *n'* (from *ne*) and *pas*; therefore, *de* does not carry any new meaning in the utterances.

Once again we ask the question: how might an instructor make use of this information in constructing SI activities for the *un/de* distinction? As we saw with the Spanish subjunctive, there are indeed ways for instructors to manipulate input so that these medial-position markers in French are relocated to a more salient position. For example, Activity G separates out the *ne* + verb + *pas* phrase from the noun phrase containing *de/d'*. In this way, learners are pushed to attend to *de/d'* (now in utterance-initial position) for meaning and complete each activity item correctly.

Activity G The LeBlanc Family

Step 1. Pierre and Lise LeBlanc are talking about things they have and don't have in their house. Pay attention to the articles to determine whether they have or do not have the things mentioned. Complete each sentence with either *Nous avons...* or *Nous n'avons pas....*

_____	*une salle de séjour.*	a living room
_____	*de télévision.*	a television
_____	*de lit.*	a bed
_____	*un fauteuil.*	an armchair
_____	*une cuisinière.*	a stove
_____	*de réfrigérateur.*	a refrigerator
_____	*une table.*	a table
_____	*une toilette.*	a toilet
_____	*une douche.*	a shower
_____	*de baignoire.*	a bathtub
_____	*de lampes.*	lamps

_____ *de chaises.*	chairs
_____ *des souris.*	mice

Step 2. Based on these descriptions, place a mark somewhere along the line below to indicate the economic status of the LeBlanc family.

Pierre et Lise LeBlanc sont....

très riches   riches   assez riches   assez pauvres   pauvres   très pauvres

⟵──⟶

very rich   rich   sufficiently rich   poor enough   poor   very poor

Step 3. Now get together with a partner and compare your ranking of the family's status with theirs. Do you both agree or disagree? Explain your answer to each other and be prepared to let the whole class know your thoughts.

(Based on materials from Wong, 2004)

Also note that this activity includes two follow-up steps for the purpose of demonstrating how an SI activity for P1f might conclude. In this particular activity, learners must draw a conclusion from the statements made with regard to a couple's economic profile. This second step serves to keep meaning in focus so that students do not simply complete the activity mechanically, disregarding what each utterance actually means. The last step involves sharing their answers with a partner and perhaps the whole class. In short, Step 1 is referential and Step 2 is affective. Note that follow-up steps such as Step 3 are sometimes central to the success of SI activities. Later in this chapter, it will be *your* job to add follow-up steps to the activities we have already discussed.

Almost any SI activity can easily include one or more follow-up steps. In the following affective activity, we see that a follow-up step may be as simple as repeating the activity in light of a new context. In Activity H, students are first asked to give their opinions based on the present day and then to give their opinions with a new context: the 1960s. Of course, once again, each activity item is structured such that the indefinite articles are located in the more salient, utterance-initial position.

Activity H   College Life

Step 1. The following sentences describe what is and what is not typically found in a college dorm room. Read each sentence and decide whether each description is typical or not typical of a college dorm room.

Aujourd'hui, une chambre d'étudiant a...		C'est typique	Ce n'est pas typique
une chaîne stéréo	a stereo	_____	_____
une télévision	a television	_____	_____
un lecteur de DVD	a DVD player	_____	_____
un four à micro-ondes	a microwave	_____	_____

Aujourd'hui, une chambre d'étudiant n'a pas...		C'est typique	Ce n'est pas typique
de lavabo	a sink	_____	_____
de cuisine	a kitchen	_____	_____
de réfrigérateur	a refrigerator	_____	_____
de radio	a radio	_____	_____

Step 2. Now, repeat the preceding activity, but this time imagine a college dorm room from the 1960s. Do any of your answers change?

En 1960, une chambre d'étudiant a...	C'est typique	Ce n'est pas typique
une chaîne stéréo.	_____	_____
une télévision.	_____	_____
un lecteur de DVD.	_____	_____
un four à micro-ondes	_____	_____

En 1960, une chambre d'étudiant n'a pas...	C'est typique	Ce n'est pas typique
de lavabo.	_____	_____
de cuisine.	_____	_____
de réfrigérateur.	_____	_____
de radio.	_____	_____

(Based on materials from Wong, 2004)

PRINCIPLES IN PRACTICE

The previous sections of this chapter serve as a useful guide for the development of further activities that push learners to overcome P1f. Now, we will work through a few tasks to prepare you for the design of your own activities:

TASK A. If you go back and look at activities A–E of this chapter, you will notice that, for each activity, there are only six to eight items given as examples. Use your creativity to see if you can add two more activity items to complete each activity. Be ready to share your activity items with your colleagues. (Write your items in English or Spanish, depending on the makeup of the group to whom you will present.)

TASK B. You may have noticed that Activities G and H included follow-up steps. When students know that they will be responsible for the content of each activity item, they are much more likely to pay attention to what each means.

Return once again to activities A–E of this chapter and, for each activity, add one or more follow-up steps that will encourage students to pay attention to what is discussed in Step 1. You may write out the instruction lines (and any items) in English if needed so that your colleagues can understand and benefit from your ideas.

TASK C. Now it's time for you to create some of your own activities. Choose a feature from the language that you teach and design two of your own SI activities—one referential and one affective. One of the activities should require listening. You may wish to review the difference between referential and affective activities before you begin working. Also, remember to adhere to these four guidelines from VanPatten (1996) that were discussed in Chapter 1 as you create your activities:

1. Present one thing (one function or use) at a time.
2. Keep meaning in focus.
3. Have learners do something with the input.
4. Keep the learner's processing strategy (in this case, P1f) in mind.

TWO SAMPLE STUDIES

In Farley (2001a), twenty-nine participants enrolled in a fourth-semester Spanish course were assigned to one of two treatments: processing instruction (PI) and meaning-based output instruction (MOI). The PI treatment consisted of eight SI activities similar to Activities A–E in this chapter and some EI about the subjunctive and the processing issues that may affect noticing and processing of the subjunctive. The MOI group also received EI about the subjunctive, but the activities they carried out were solely production-oriented. Note that the PI group *never produced* a single subjunctive form at any time during the treatment. They only interpreted the SI containing subjunctives. In contrast, the MOI group only produced subjunctives.

The purpose of Farley (2001a) was to investigate whether or not PI and/or MOI would bring about improved performance on sentence-level tasks involving the interpretation and production of the Spanish subjunctive and whether the improvement would be equal for both types of instruction. The results of Farley (2001a) are provided in Table 3.2. The results of Farley (2001a) indicate that PI (SI + EI) had an overall greater effect than the meaning-based output group. The group that received SI improved more than the other group on the interpretation task and produced just as well as the output-focused group. Getting the SI resulted in some type of internalization in the learners' developing systems that led to an improvement, not only in interpretation, but in production as well. The output-based treatment did not have nearly the effect on interpretation that the PI treatment did. The output-focused activities did have an effect on what learners were able to produce, but this effect was no greater than the SI's influence on production. In short, the group that received no production practice appears to have received what they needed (SI) in order to produce as well as the group that received only production practice.

Why did the output-based treatment result in any improvement on the interpretation task? Good question. These results may be due to learner output

TABLE 3.2 Mean Score and Standard Deviation on Interpretation and Production Tasks for the PI and MOI Groups in Farley (2001a)

Task	Processing Instruction ($n = 17$)		Meaning-Based Output Instruction ($n = 12$)	
	Mean	SD	Mean	SD
Interpretation Task				
Pre-test	3.18	1.29	2.83	1.11
Immediate Post-test	6.82	1.47	5.50	2.39
Two-week Post-test	6.65	1.93	3.92	3.12
Production Task				
Pre-test	.88	1.65	.33	.89
Immediate Post-test	6.18	2.16	6.33	2.06
Two-week Post-test	6.18	2.46	5.25	3.22

being utilized as incidental SI for other learners. That is, during the follow-up step to each activity, when the instructor asked students to give an answer to an activity item, the students' answer (when correct) served as incidental aural input for those who were listening. The results of Farley (2001a) highlight the important role of input in SLA and the benefits of PI in particular. Read more about this study in the May 2001 issue of the journal *Hispania*.

Farley (2001b) also examined the relative effects of SI activities and meaning-based output activities on learner performance during sentence-level interpretation and production tasks involving the Spanish subjunctive. Fifty participants were administered either ten SI activities or ten meaning-based output activities. In addition, both treatment groups received a grammatical explanation and some hints concerning the difficulty in processing the redundant (P1a), embedded (P1f) subjunctive markers. As in Farley (2001a), the PI group never produced any subjunctives during the treatment, and the MOI group produced *only* subjunctives (never interpreting SI). The results of Farley (2001b) are provided in Table 3.3.

TABLE 3.3 Mean Score and Standard Deviation on Interpretation and Production Tasks for the PI and MOI Groups in Farley (2001b)

Task	Processing Instruction ($n = 24$)		Meaning-Based Output Instruction ($n = 26$)	
	Mean	SD	Mean	SD
Interpretation Task				
Pre-test	3.21	1.14	3.58	1.24
Immediate Post-test	6.54	1.74	7.04	1.82
Two-week Post-test	6.83	1.90	6.69	2.00
Production Task				
Pre-test	0.17	0.46	0.33	0.66
Immediate Post-test	4.29	1.68	4.12	1.73
Two-week Post-test	3.63	1.67	3.81	1.74

The results of Farley (2001b) revealed that both instruction types brought about improved performance on both tasks, and the performance of both treatment groups was statistically similar in every respect. In this study, the learners were enrolled in an intensive track, and more activities were provided (ten instead of eight). In addition, the effects proved durable two weeks after instruction. You can read more about this study in the December 2001 issue of *Spanish Applied Linguistics* or in Chapter 7 of the book entitled *Processing Instruction* published by Erlbaum Press, 2004.

READ MORE ABOUT IT

Collentine, J.G. (1998). Processing instruction and the subjunctive. *Hispania* 81, 576–587.

Farley, A.P. (2002). Processing instruction, communicative value, and ecological validity: A response to Collentine's defense. *Hispania*, 85: 889–895.

Farley, A. (2001a). Authentic processing instruction and the Spanish subjunctive. *Hispania* 84: 289–299.

Farley, A. (2001b). Processing instruction and meaning-based output instruction: A comparative study. *Spanish Applied Linguistics.* December, 2001.

Wong, W. (2002). Linking form and meaning: Processing instruction. *The French Review* 76: 2.

The First Noun Principle

INTRODUCTION

Read the following six sentences and for each decide who called whom.

Ellen called him.

*Him called Ellen.

*Ellen him called.

*Him Ellen called.

*Called him Ellen.

*Called Ellen him.

It is quite easy to determine who did the calling and who answered the phone in most of these utterances, yet English allows only one of these sentences. All the starred utterances are ungrammatical in English, but in many other languages (such as the Romance languages) some of these word orders would be perfectly acceptable. How do speakers of these other languages know who is doing what to whom? Easy. The word *him* is an object pronoun and *him* always receives the phone call regardless of the word order used to express the action.

In an earlier chapter we briefly discussed the idea that grammatical form exists at the sentence level too, not just at the word or morphological level. As an input string (written or aural) gets processed by an L2 learner, the recipient of the input must naturally assign roles to each noun or pronoun in the string, deciding who or what is doing the action (or which word is the agent) and who or what is not doing the action.

Research on L2 input processing indicates that learners tend to assign the role of subject or agent to the first noun that they encounter in an input string. When this tendency is exhibited, it sometimes results in a successful assigning of semantic roles and sometimes it does not. Of course, the English language mandates an obligatory subject-verb-object (SVO) word order, and therefore learners who exhibit a tendency to make the first noun the subject receive confirmation from English. But what about other languages that allow for more flexible word order, permitting OVS or even VOS in addition to SVO? When an L2 learner is attempting to acquire any of these languages, we see that this tendency, which VanPatten (2004) calls the First Noun Principle, is certainly less than optimal. In fact, even passive utterances in English such as *the man was visited by his grandson* are sometimes misinterpreted as active utterances (in this case, *the man visited his grandson*) by ESL learners.

You probably recall from Chapter 1 that there are times that the FNP tends to be overridden: (1) when lexical semantics comes into play; (2) when an interpretation of an utterance is not very probable; and (3) when context pushes L2 learners toward one interpretation over another. First, the meaning of a given word all by itself can influence the assignment of roles that a learner gravitates toward. For instance, compare the following pair of utterances.

> *Greg was visited by many people.*
> *The museum was visited by many people.*

Even though both utterances are passive constructions, the first is much more likely to be misinterpreted as an active construction than the second. This is simply due to lexical semantics—that is, the meaning of the first noun that learners encounter.

The probability that an event took place (or might hypothetically take place) also influences the "strength" of the FNP during on-line comprehension. If a given role assignment is not likely (with regard to the event occurring in that way), then L2 learners will naturally abort the FNP and assign semantic roles that seem plausible. For example, consider the utterance:

> *Dave was promoted by his boss.*

It is unlikely that anyone would be in the situation of promoting their own boss. Hence, in this instance, it is much less likely that ESL learners would resort to the FNP and interpret this utterance to mean *Dave promoted his boss*.

Finally, context can certainly influence the interpretation of a given utterance. Imagine that the following utterance stood alone in the input:

> *The veteran was worried by the young rookie.*

This utterance all by itself might be easily misinterpreted by ESL learners to mean *The veteran worried the young rookie*. However, what if the utterance was embedded in the following context?

> *His best years were behind him now, and so many new players were arriving. With little time left in his career, the Hall of Famer was afraid he'd soon be replaced. Naturally, the veteran was worried by the young rookie.*

This same utterance, when accompanied by a constraining context, is now much less likely to be misinterpreted as *the veteran worried the young rookie*. Hence, although the tendency to rely on the FNP is normally strong, we have seen three instances in which reliance on the FNP is attenuated.

Principle 2.   The First Noun Principle. Learners tend to process the first noun or pronoun they encounter in a sentence as the subject/agent.

> P2a. *The Lexical Semantics Principle.* Learners may rely on lexical semantics, where possible, instead of word order to interpret sentences.
>
> P2b. *The Event Probabilities Principle.* Learners may rely on event probabilities, where possible, instead of word order to interpret sentences.
>
> P2c. *The Contextual Constraint Principle.* Learners may rely less on the FNP if preceding context constrains the possible interpretation of a clause or sentence.
>
> VanPatten (2004)

GRAMMATICAL FORMS AFFECTED BY PRINCIPLE 2

What grammatical forms might be affected by the FNP? Table 4.1 lists some of the language features from five different languages that can be affected in some way by the FNP.

You can easily see that the structures that tend to interact with Principle 2 are object pronouns, case markers, and passive constructions. In short, any feature that helps communicate who did what to whom can undergo a delay in processing due to FNP influence.

THE FIRST NOUN PRINCIPLE: SOME RESEARCH

You might think that the FNP is a tendency caused by the interference of English or other first languages. However, the FNP has been evidenced in L2 learners with a number of different native languages that have varying rules about word order. For example, Ervin-Tripp (1974) investigated the tendencies of native speakers of English who interpreted passive constructions in their second language, French. In this study, child participants acted out the meaning of passive utterances using toy animals. Ervin-Tripp found that the children consistently acted out the opposite of each utterance's true meaning. That is, when one animal was described as biting, eating, or chasing the other, the children instead portrayed the "victim" biting, eating, or chasing the assailant. The learners consistently assigned the role of agent to the first noun that they encountered in an input string. Hence, passives were misunderstood as active constructions. These results held for younger as well as older children who knew and could use passives in their native language, English. If this learner tendency were simply a product of first language interference, then the FNP would not have been evidenced in Ervin-Tripp's study.

LoCoco (1987) investigated L2 German learners' interpretation of German OVS utterances. LoCoco found that L2 learners of German tended to skip over case markers and assign semantic roles via word order when the object came before the verb. Instructional intervention by way of explicit teaching on

TABLE 4.1 Some Language Features Affected by Principle 2

Spanish	French	Italian	English (ESL)	German
Word order	Word order	Word order		Word order
Passive constructions	Passive constructions	Passive constructions	Passive constructions	Passive constructions
Case marker	Case marker	Case marker		Case marker
Object pronouns	Object pronouns	Object pronouns		Object pronouns

German word order and case markers did not prevent learners from assuming that the first noun in the input string was the subject. Gass's (1989) study resulted in similar findings for L2 Italian and ESL. In Nam (1975), ESL learners whose native language was Korean also incorrectly interpreted passive constructions as actives. Finally, McDonald and Heilenman (1992) found that L2 learners of French whose native language was English used the FNP to determine who was doing what to whom. One might speculate from this trend in results that there is some innate predisposition in every human being, regardless of their L1, that leans them toward SVO/SOV word order. We see the FNP in action not only with L2 processing but also in first language acquisition. For example, Pléh (1989), in studying 178 child (L1) learners of Hungarian, found that they consistently tended to assign the role of agent to the first noun that they encountered in the input string.

Now, we have seen that the FNP is a psycholinguistic reality. That is, it does influence both L1 and L2 learner processing. However, does research show that the FNP always influences on-line comprehension to the same degree? Absolutely not. You recall that three factors (lexical semantics, event probability, and contextual constraints) can affect the degree to which the FNP is employed. Research on both L1 and L2 processing bears this out. For example, Bavin and Shopen (1989) examined the interpretation processes of L1 learners of Warlpiri, an Aboriginal language of Australia that has free word order. Warlpiri, like Sanskrit and some other languages, allows utterances with any possible word order: SVO, OVS, VOS, VSO, SOV, or OSV, not to mention the variances allowed when adjuncts are involved. Bavin and Shopen found that the children relied on the FNP when the action (verb) took either an animate or inanimate object. However, when the action could be performed only by an animate entity, the children consistently relied on both lexical semantics and event probability to interpret these active sentences in Warlpiri. Gass (1989) gave L2 learners of English and L2 learners of Italian utterances in which verbs that could take only an animate subject were preceded by inanimate nouns. That is, utterances were of the following type: *The tree climbed the bear.* Gass found that both groups of learners exhibited strong tendencies to rely on lexical semantics rather than word order when interpreting this type of utterance. In Issidorides and Hulstijn (1992), L2 learners of Dutch who came from several different L1 backgrounds exhibited a tendency to rely on the FNP for interpreting utterances of VSO word order except when the first noun in the utterance was inanimate and the second was animate. Finally, in VanPatten and Houston (1998), L2 learners of Spanish showed less or no reliance on the FNP when the utterance they interpreted carried a constraining context.

Pause to consider...

how the FNP might affect students of the language that you teach. If your language of instruction is included in Table 4.1, go back and review the features listed there. Are you able to come up with a sample utterance that might be misinterpreted? How about one in which lexical semantics or event probability might come into play?

EXAMPLE 1: OBJECT PRONOUNS IN SPANISH

In Spanish, direct object pronouns such as *me* 'me,' *te* 'you,' and *la* 'her' precede the verb in most instances. In addition, Spanish allows for somewhat flexible word order in that subjects can appear after the verb. This means that both of the following constructions are possible in Spanish to communicate the *same* meaning:

Juan la respeta.	lit: *John her respects.*	meaning: *John respects her.*
La respeta Juan.	lit: *Her respects John.*	meaning: *John respects her.*

Spanish also marks the accusative noun phrase (NP) with a personal *a* case marker when lexical semantics permit the NP to hypothetically be the agent.

You can probably guess by now what the processing problem is regarding the FNP for L2 learners of Spanish. When they hear or read *La respeta Juan* (literally, *her-respects-John*), what might they think it means? If you answered *She respects John,* then you are right. The pronoun *la* may be misinterpreted as the subject *she* since it is the first noun or pronoun they encounter in the utterance.

Now, for the third time in this book we arrive at a logical question: is there a psycholinguistically motivated grammar instruction that can help with this learner processing problem? The answer is yes. As with the Primacy of Meaning Principle and the Sentence Location Principle, activity items can be fashioned in such a way as to push learners away from their dependency on the FNP for subject-agent role assignment. We will now look at some SI activities in Spanish (and later in German) that take Principle 2 into account. When designing referential SI activities to help learners avoid reliance on the FNP, there are two designs that work best. The first involves the use of photos, drawings, or images of some type, whereas the second involves the use of English (or L1) translations. In this section, we will take a look at both designs.

In Activity A, the instructions are quite simple, and the task involves picture selection. Here, L2 learners of Spanish listen to a variety of utterances presented in either SVO or OVS word order. Note that in Activity A, the items alternate between OVS (items 1 and 3) and SVO (items 2 and 4). This is a deliberate attempt to push learners away from the assumption that input will always come their way in SVO word order. During the follow-up in which learners receive feedback regarding the correct answer (when they are simply told that a or b is correct), their FNP-based hypotheses will be confirmed at times and called into question other times. This is the purpose of structuring the input in this way.

Activity A demonstrates how drawings (or images of any kind) can be used for SI activities that take Principle 2 into account. However, interpretation options do not have to be represented pictorially. They might simply be expressed in the L1, as shown in Activity B.

Activity A   A Lover's Quarrel in Destinos

Although they don't show it on camera, Arturo and Raquel often quarrel and misunderstand each other. You will hear some sentences in Spanish describing their interactions. Select the correct picture for each statement made.

1.   ☐ a   ☐ b

2.   ☐ a   ☐ b

3.   ☐ a   ☐ b

4. ☐ a ☐ b

[more activity items of the same format]

INSTRUCTOR'S SCRIPT

1. *No la cree Arturo.*	Arturo doesn't believe her.
2. *Raquel no lo cree.*	Raquel doesn't believe him.
3. *Lo sigue Raquel.*	Raquel follows him.
4. *Arturo sigue a Raquel.*	Arturo follows Raquel.

(drawings taken from VanPatten & Cadierno, 1993)

Both Activity A and Activity B are referential in nature in that the items have only one right answer. Activity A provides oral input, whereas Activity B involves interpreting written input. Activity A depicts actions via drawings, whereas Activity B does so via the use of English. Despite these differences, both activities have the same objective—to show learners that the FNP does fail them.

Activity B Bart and His Mom

You have probably caught at least one episode of *The Simpsons* while channel surfing, and you know that Bart is not exactly the role model for all youth. He must drive his mother Marge crazy! Still, Bart is not all that bad, and he loves his mom. Read each statement below about Bart and his mom and decide which English renditions accurately represent the Spanish.

1. *No la comprende Bart.*
a. She doesn't understand Bart.
b. Bart doesn't understand her.

2. *Bart la besa.*
a. She kisses Bart.
b. Bart kisses her.

3. *Lo abraza Marge.*
a. Marge hugs him.
b. He hugs Marge.

4. *Marge lo sorprende.*
a. Marge surprises him.
b. He surprises Marge.

[more activity items of the same format]

Now we will look at two affective activities for object pronouns in Spanish. In Activity C, learners read very short utterances about a relative and respond to the input, making decisions about which items apply to them.

Activity C   How Do You Feel About Your Relatives?

Step 1. Select a female relative of yours and write her name and relationship below: *madre* (mother), *hermana* (sister), *tía* (aunt), *abuela* (grandmother), *prima* (cousin), and so on. Which of the statements describes how you feel about her?

Pariente: _____   *Nombre:* _____

Relative   Name

_____ **1.** *La admiro.*   I admire her.

_____ **2.** *La respeto.*   I respect her.

_____ **3.** *La quiero mucho.*   I love her dearly.

_____ **4.** *La imito.*   I imitate her.

_____ **5.** *La detesto.*   I detest her.

_____ **6.** *La* _____ .   I _____ .

Step 2. Now select a male relative: *padre* (father), *hermano* (brother), *tío* (uncle), *abuelo* (grandfather), *primo* (cousin), and so on, write his name and relationship, and indicate which statements describe your feelings about him.

Pariente: _____   *Nombre:* _____

Relative   Name

_____ **1.** *Lo admiro.*   I admire him.

_____ **2.** *Lo respeto.*   I respect him.

_____ **3.** *Lo quiero mucho.*   I love him dearly.

_____ **4.** *Lo imito.*   I imitate him.

_____ **5.** *Lo detesto.*   I detest him.

_____ **6.** *Lo* _____ .   I _____ .

Step 3. Compare your answers with two other people. Did you select the same relative(s)? Did you mark the same items?

(adapted from VanPatten & Cadierno, 1993)

Did you notice where the object pronouns tend to appear in the last few activities? You probably remember the Sentence Location Principle from the last chapter that states that utterance-initial position is the most salient. In these activities, not only are learners pushed to "give up" on the FNP, but also the form in focus (the pronouns *lo/la*) appears at the beginning whenever possible. This is yet another example of how more than one principle can interact with a grammatical structure, and how instructors must keep *all* relevant learner processing strategies in mind when they design an activity. Did you also notice that all the activities in this section limit the presentation of object pronouns to third person singular forms only? In this way, the activities follow VanPatten's (1996) guideline: *present one thing at a time.*

Before we move on to look at SI activities for German, we will look at one more affective activity, Activity D.

Activity D   My Best Friends

Step 1. Indicate whether or not each statement about your best male friend applies to you.

Mi mejor amigo se llama _____ .

My best (male) friend's name is_____ .

	Sí, me aplica. Yes, it applies to me.	*No, no me aplica.* No, it doesn't apply.
1. *Lo llamo con frecuencia.* I call him frequently.	————	————
2. *Lo abrazo cuando lo veo.* I give him a hug when I see him.	————	————
3. *Lo comprendo muy bien.* I understand him very well.	————	————
4. *Lo visito a veces.* I visit him sometimes.	————	————
5. *Lo aprecio mucho.* I appreciate him a lot.	————	————

Step 2. Indicate whether the same statements apply for your best female friend.

Mi mejor amiga se llama: _____ .

My best (female) friend's name is: _____ .

	Sí, me aplica. Yes, it applies to me.	*No, no me aplica.* No, it doesn't apply.
1. *La llamo con frecuencia.* I call her frequently.	————	————
2. *La abrazo cuando la veo.* I give her a hug when I see her.	————	————
3. *La comprendo muy bien.* I understand her very well.	————	————

4. *La visito a veces.*

   I visit her sometimes.   _____   _____

5. *La aprecio mucho.*

   I appreciate her a lot.   _____   _____

Step 3. Did you answer any question in Step 2 differently from the same question in Step 1? How many did you answer differently?

Step 4. How would you describe your relationship with these two friends? Be ready to tell a partner what you decided and explain why.

   a. very similar
   b. somewhat different
   c. very different

(adapted from VanPatten & Cadierno, 1993)

Activity D is a good example of an SI activity that has several steps and follow-up phases. After learners respond to the input concerning two friends (one male and one female), Step 3 asks them to compare their answers to Steps 1 and 2. This comparison then serves as material for reflection and discussion in Step 4. The instructor might even poll the students as a whole after Step 4 to look for trends in their responses. As I have stressed before in this book, follow-up steps can go a long way in making SI activities more interesting. They may cause learners to pay more attention to the input, since learners quickly see that they will be responsible for their responses during a second, third, or fourth step.

All human languages express actions, have subjects (explicit or nonexplicit), and are capable of communicating who did what to whom. Therefore, the four activities that you have just seen can easily be adapted to nearly any, if not all, languages. You can probably imagine fairly easily how Activities A, B, C, and D could work for English passives (for example, *Arturo was followed by Raquel*) or OVS constructions in the language that you teach. It is easy to incorporate images, L1 translations, and VanPatten's SI guidelines into the design of FNP-focused SI activities for Romance languages, Germanic languages, and many other languages. To illustrate this briefly, we will end this section by looking at two activities for German.

EXAMPLE 2: OBJECT PRONOUNS IN GERMAN

German maintains a fairly strict word order, although not nearly as rigid as the English SVO-only rule. In German, the verb carrying tense must be in position two in the utterance. When an auxiliary verb marking tense is present, the auxiliary comes second in the utterance and the other verb(s) is (are) found in utterance-final position. German does allow for both OVS (object-verb-subject) and SVO (subject-verb-object) word orders in main clauses since the only rule to which an utterance must adhere is that the tense-marking verb should appear second. Still, SVO is much more frequently used than OVS. SOV and OSV are generally prohibited (in main clauses) since both orders violate the tense-marking-verb-is-second rule.

The processing problem that L2 learners of German encounter with object pronouns is that they will tend to assign the role of subject or agent to the accusative pronoun in the input. As with Spanish, we are obviously referring to the FNP again. Since SVO is more frequent in the input, most of the time their hypothesis is only supported, whereas the truth of the matter is that the FNP is not always optimal since OVS can and does appear. Unless learners of German are exposed to a significant amount of input of the OVS nature, they can "get by" in using the FNP. That is, they can rely solely on word order to tell them who did what to whom and simply fail to notice or process the difference between the nominative *er* 'he' and the accusative *ihn* 'him.' Note that when a female is mentioned together with either masculine pronoun (nominative or accusative) it does not help learners decipher who is doing the action since *she* and *her* have the same form (*sie*) in German. L2 learners of German must learn to differentiate between the subject pronoun *er* and the object pronoun *ihn* to know who is doing what to whom. This is where SI can help. Just as we saw in the SI activities for object pronouns in Spanish, German input can also be structured in such a way that learners will become aware that the FNP is not entirely reliable and that they need to look to other cues in the input to assign semantic roles.

Activity E   People Watching

Sometimes it's fun to sit in the park and just "people watch." Human interactions can be so fascinating, and you can learn a lot about what makes people in general "tick." Listen to each statement and select the scene that matches what you hear.

1.

2.

INSTRUCTOR'S SCRIPT
1. *Er hört sie zu.*
lit: he listens her to
(SVO)

2. *Sie sieht er.*
lit: her watches he
(OVS)

3.

4.

INSTRUCTOR'S SCRIPT

3. *Ihn hört sie.*
lit: him hears she
(SVO)

4. *Ihn grüßt sie.*
lit: him greets she
(OVS)

[more activity items of the same format]

(drawings taken from VanPatten & Cadierno, 1993)

Activity E once again illustrates how interpretation options (a or b) can be represented pictorially. Here, learners listen to each utterance and select the image that correctly depicts the action. Recall that the feminine pronouns are no giveaway since the form *sie* is both nominative and accusative. If learners are to succeed here, they must notice and process the meaning of *ihn* (in contrast to *er*).

This activity in its entirety might contain seven to ten utterances with four to seven of them being of OVS word order. If SVO is of much higher frequency in natural input, it is only logical that SI be fashioned to do what raw input cannot do as effectively—show learners how the FNP fails. Having more OVS activity items than SVO items maximizes the effectiveness of referential activities for the FNP-related language features.

In Activity F, we see both a referential phase and an affective phase centered on the same theme: Andre Agassi and Steffi Graf. First, learners make a decision about who does what to whom merely by checking a space designated for Agassi or Graf. In all the previous activities that we have seen, either pictures or L1 translations were used as potential answers. A third option is illustrated here in that learners simply select the "doer" of the action as an indication of correct utterance interpretation.

In the second phase, learners express their opinion about the most important ingredients in a healthy relationship. Since this phase is affective, *all* the items appear in OVS word order. Remember that affective activities serve as reinforcement after referential activities have induced form-meaning connections. Finally, in Step 3, learners compare their responses to the affective items with those of a classmate, and they prepare to potentially report their comparison during a whole-class discussion.

Activity F   Andre and Steffi

Andre Agassi and Steffi Graf are professional tennis players, marriage partners, and parents. Andre's resurgence on tour have been due to Steffi's support, but he supports her in many ways as well.

Step 1. Listen to the following descriptions of their relationship and decide who is doing the action.

	Andre	Steffi	INSTRUCTOR'S SCRIPT	
1.	_____	_____	*Sie versteht ihn.*	She understands him. (SVO)
2.	_____	_____	*Er stützt sie.*	He supports her. (SVO)
3.	_____	_____	*Ihn liebt sie.*	She loves him. (OVS)
4.	_____	_____	*Sie sieht er.*	He watches her. (OVS)
5.	_____	_____	*Ihn spielt sie.*	She plays him. (OVS)

[more activity items of the same format]

Step 2. Even though Steffi is a super spouse, decide which of her caring actions are absolute essentials for a good marriage by ranking each from most important (1) to least important (7). Feel free to give more than one item the same ranking.

Ranking   Action

_____	*Ihn liebt sie.*	She loves him. (OVS)
_____	*Ihn spielt sie.*	She plays him. (OVS)
_____	*Ihn versteht sie.*	She understands him. (OVS)
_____	*Ihn umarmt sie.*	She hugs him. (OVS)
_____	*Ihn stützt sie.*	She supports him. (OVS)
_____	*Ihn sieht sie.*	She watches him. (OVS)
_____	*Ihn hört sie zu.*	She listens to him. (OVS)

Step 3. Compare your responses with a partner. Did you tend to agree about the most essential qualities in a good spouse? Be ready to report your findings to the class.

Now that you have had the opportunity to see SI activities combat the FNP in two very different languages, are you ready to begin designing some of your own activities? Let's find out. In this next section, you'll be asked to do just that.

This chapter serves as a guide for the development of SI activities that push learners to avoid reliance on Principle 2. Now we will work through some tasks that will conclude with the design of your own activities.

TASK A. At the beginning of this chapter, you read a discussion of Principle 2 and its three subprinciples. Now write two sentences in the language that you teach in which the FNP would fail learners. Then write one sentence in which P2a would come into play and one sentence in which P2b would be a factor. Finally, take one of your two sentences (for Principle 2) and write a constraining context that would attenuate the influence of the FNP.

TASK B. Now it's time to get creative. See if you can come up with a fun and interesting context in which students can decide who did what to whom in the language that you teach. You may wish to go back and review the Andre Agassi and Steffi Graf activity to get your ideas flowing. Try to think of at least one original idea for a referential activity and one for an affective activity. It may be helpful to do this task with a partner. You do not have to design the activity. Just explain the over-arching theme and decision that learners must make.

TASK C. Choose a feature from the language that you teach that is affected by the FNP and design two of your own SI activities—one referential and one affective. One of the activities should involve images while the other should involve L1 translations or choosing the "doer." You may want to go back and review the activities in this chapter first. Be sure to include at least one follow-up step for the affective activity.

THREE SAMPLE STUDIES

VanPatten and Cadierno (1993) was the first study that compared the effects of processing instruction (SI + EI) with those of traditional instruction. The study was based on the FNP, which (to review) explains why many learners of Spanish interpret sentences such as *Lo llama la chica* as "He calls the girl," when in fact *lo* is an object pronoun and the correct interpretation is "The girl calls him." Therefore, VanPatten and Cadierno (1993) often placed the subjects at the end of each sentence. The SI activities in their study attempted to reorganize the interpretation strategies of the learners, so that they took notice of how each utterance was organized syntactically.

There were three groups of subjects: (1) a control group that received no instruction on object pronouns; (2) a group that received traditional instruction that included a grammatical explanation (EI), oral and written mechanical drills, meaningful drills, and communicative activities; and (3) a group that received processing instruction (EI + SI). The last group received SI activities designed to counteract the FNP exactly like those illustrated in this chapter and were never asked to produce any object pronouns at all.

The results suggest that PI has a greater effect on the acquisition of object pronouns (and Spanish word order) than traditional instruction, which focuses on language production. Learners who received PI outperformed the other two groups on the interpretation task, and the results of the production task showed no significant difference between the PI group and the traditional instruction group, with both outperforming the control group. The fact that the PI group performed just as well on the production task helped to solidify the claim that altering a learner's processing strategies can affect their developing system.

VanPatten and Sanz (1995) investigated the effects of PI on oral language production, using the same grammatical focus as that of VanPatten and Cadierno (1993), namely object pronouns in Spanish. The subjects were divided into two groups: (1) those who received PI, and (2) the control group that received no instruction. The pre-test and post-test consisted of three tasks: a sentence-level task, a video-narration task, and a question-answer task. Each task had both an oral and a written version. VanPatten and Sanz found that PI yielded beneficial effects not only for written language production but also for oral language production. The PI group performed significantly better on all three tasks after the treatment, whereas the control group showed no significant improvement. The greatest improvements after treatment were evidenced on the video-narration and sentence-level tasks, where the processing group performed better on the written versions of each task. There was no significant difference, however, between the written and oral versions of the question-answer task. In summary, those who received PI made significant gains on all three tasks in the written mode, and two of the three oral tasks. VanPatten and Sanz's study was crucial in that it showed for the first time that PI resulted in improvement on both oral and written language tasks.

VanPatten and Oikennon (1996) conducted a study to determine whether the gains made by those receiving PI might be attributed to the EI given as part of PI or whether it was the SI activities alone that produced the results. Subjects were divided into three groups: (1) those who received EI only, (2) those who received SI activities, and (3) those who received both EI and SI activities. The results indicated that the structured input–only group performed significantly better on both post-tests (consisting of an interpretation task and a production task) than the EI-only group. There was no difference between the SI-only group and the SI + EI group. Also, the EI-only group showed no significant improvement after treatment.

READ MORE ABOUT IT

VanPatten, B., & Cadierno, T. (1993). Input processing and second language acquisition: A role for instruction. *Modern Language Journal* 77: 45–57.

VanPatten, B., & Oikennon, S. (1996). Explanation versus structured input in processing instruction. *Studies in Second Language Acquisition* 18: 495–510.

VanPatten, B., & Sanz, C. (1995). From input to output: Processing instruction and communicative tasks. In F. Eckman, D. Highland, P. W. Lee, J. Mileham, & R. R. Weber (eds.), *Second Language Acquisition Theory and Pedagogy* (169–185). Hillsdale, NJ: Erlbaum.

CHAPTER 5

SI Activity Design: Common Pitfalls and Frequently Asked Questions

INTRODUCTION

An instructor who has little or no previous experience with SI activities will inevitably encounter particular difficulties and have certain questions about activity design. In this chapter, I examine some of the most common pitfalls, and discuss how a designer of SI activities might avoid them. The first six pitfalls that I discuss relate directly to *not* following the guidelines for designing SI activities as given in VanPatten (1996); the second set of pitfalls are other problems that frequently arise when instructors misunderstand the nature and the goal of SI activities. Then, in the second half of this chapter, I address some frequently asked questions about SI activity design.

PART 1: COMMON PITFALLS

The goal of this first section is to review some of the basic guidelines of activity design and provide further help to those who are just beginning to create their own SI instructional materials. Let's begin by revisiting VanPatten's guidelines and discuss some of the pitfalls of not following them.

Pitfall #1: Not presenting one thing at a time.

As you have seen throughout this book, SI activities have consistently presented one form or structure at a time. For example, in the activities for the future tense in Italian and the subjunctive in Spanish, you probably noticed that the sample activity items presented only first person singular forms for Italian and third person singular forms for Spanish. This was no coincidence, since one of the VanPatten (1996) guidelines for SI activity design is to teach only one thing at a time. In minimizing the "learner load" by focusing on only one form during an activity or series of activities, learners are more likely to process that form. A common temptation for language instructors, however, is to "teach" as much as they know as early as possible. The underlying assumption of this approach is that the more forms you present, the more learners will acquire. This assumption might lead to an activity for the future tense in English (ESL) such as Activity A.

Activity A The Future

Read each statement about the future and decide whether each is probable or improbable for the year 2030.

Probable	Improbable	In the year 2030 . . .
_____	_____	1. They will invent a flying car.
_____	_____	2. I will be married with kids.
_____	_____	3. We will have more terrorism.
_____	_____	4. The president will be a woman.

Notice how more than one form (first and third person, as well as singular and plural forms) are presented at once in this activity. In English, the word *will* is simply added to each verb, but in many other languages, as you know, each person or number carries a different form. At first glance, the approach shown in Activity A is attractive to instructors, because it seems more comprehensive and "quicker." Instructors often comment upon hearing about the one-thing-at-a-time guideline that they think it would be more efficient to present the paradigm as well as activities that introduce all forms at once. However, efficiency is a deceptive concept, because although it is true that with the multiform approach the material is *presented* more quickly, this certainly does not mean that forms are *acquired* more efficiently.

Since we have as our goal that learners make form-meaning connections, we must consider which approach will lead to the fewest incorrect form-meaning mappings. If learners are to juggle four, five, or even six forms at once, they are more likely to attribute the wrong meaning to a given form. If the meaning of a form is not interpreted correctly, obviously this can delay acquisition of that form. Logically, if a lesson and a series of sequential activities within that lesson are limited to focusing on one thing, then learners are much more likely to map the correct meaning onto the forms they listen to and read.

If an instructor who uses the traditional all-at-once approach finds that learners have not correctly processed and produced all six forms in a paradigm after six class days of practice anyway, then certainly using the one-at-a-time approach is no less efficient in the longer term. In my own teaching experience, learners who receive both explanation and practice for all forms during one lesson actually take longer to acquire and produce the target forms accurately than do those who get SI with the one-form-at-a-time approach. That is, although learners who receive SI focus only on one (or sometimes two) forms during one 50-minute period, by the end of five or six class days, they are better off than those who have been wrestling with all six forms throughout the six days. Note that VanPatten (1996) confirms similar time consumption for both approaches to form presentation in two published studies. Speaking of presenting one thing at a time, VanPatten states:

> In VanPatten and Cadierno (1993) and Cadierno (1995) this is precisely what was done—and the length of the lesson was not increased when compared to time spent on explanation and practice during traditional instruction; "full coverage" of the grammatical points was attained in both traditional and processing instruction in the same amount of time.
>
> (VanPatten, 1996, p. 67)

To clarify, this does not mean that a paradigm cannot or should not be presented to learners at the beginning of a series of class days devoted to a set of forms. Lee and VanPatten (2003) are quick to point out that paradigms can and do serve an affective function in that they satisfy a psychological or emotional need to know where the week's lesson is eventually headed. Paradigms may also help learners psychologically in that they summarize or look back on a series of lessons. Although paradigms do not accurately represent the layout of form-meaning connections in a learner's head, they are still of value to some types of learners. Hence, an instructor might briefly present the paradigm and then focus on one form within the paradigm for the first series of activities. From there, the instructor could give learners SI activities for the other forms one by one throughout a week of instruction. At the end of this week, the instructor might feel the need to summarize where the class has been by briefly reviewing the list of forms again. At best, this is how a paradigm might effectively be used along with SI activities.

Pause to consider...

how long it generally takes a learner to acquire and subsequently produce all the forms in a given paradigm. If you were to present six forms at once to learners, would they be able to interpret and produce correctly all six forms that very day? Would they retain their knowledge and abilities six days later? By presenting one form each day (or two at most), learners read and hear dozens of examples, in context, of the same form, in the same class period. At the end of six days of this focused, sequential presentation of SI, do you think learners are less likely or more likely to retain all of the forms than with the traditional all-at-once approach?

Pitfall #2: Not keeping meaning in focus.

It is a common misconception to think that SI activities are merely for "practicing grammar." Instructors often miss the fact that each activity should have its own theme that relates to a chapter or lesson theme. This also means that individual activity items should not stand alone as unrelated to other items in a given activity. Rather, all activity items should be interrelated and in some way refer back to the central theme of the activity. This will help instructors to keep meaning in focus and avoid designing mechanical, "grammar-driven" exercises. Activity B is an example of how some activity designers might fall into this pitfall of neglecting meaning and context in order to simply promote interpretation practice for its own sake.

Notice how with an activity of this type, there is no cohesive theme, no title that might bring the items together under one thematic umbrella. What ensues from a format like this is that learners quickly deduce that the instructor cares only about form, not meaning. In contrast, Activity C communicates something entirely different to the learner simply by containing a few important elements: an overarching theme, a title, and activity items that all relate to the theme and the title. Note too that even the instruction line is meaning-focused, not merely requiring learners to "choose the correct answer."

Activity B Past or Present?

Indicate whether each statement refers to a past event or a present action that happens often.

Past   Present

_____ _____   **1.** Salma Hayek went to the Oscars.

_____ _____   **2.** Michael Jordan retired from basketball.

_____ _____   **3.** Lance Armstrong wins the Tour de France.

_____ _____   **4.** Annika Sorenstam plays golf a lot.

_____ _____   **5.** Elizabeth Taylor married again.

[more activity items of the same format]

Activity C Bill Clinton: Before and After

A recent newspaper article discussed Bill Clinton's presidency and his retirement from the White House. Decide whether each excerpt taken from the article refers to Bill Clinton's life during or after his.

As President   Now   Bill Clinton . . .

_____ _____   **1.** . . . speaks at universities.

_____ _____   **2.** . . . jogged almost every day.

_____ _____   **3.** . . . met with world leaders.

_____ _____   **4.** . . . spends time with his family.

[more activity items of the same format]

An additional benefit of having one central theme is that it enables the activity designer to more easily separate out the subject and place the target (verb) form in the more salient initial position to help learners process it.

Pitfall #3: Not having learners do something with the input.

Nothing is more trivial or meaningless for a language learner than listening to L2 input simply because the class is required to do so. Input-focused activities can become especially repetitive and boring for learners if they are not asked to do something with the input. This is one of the principal characteristics that separates SI activities in particular from other input-based approaches to focus-on-form. The purpose of SI activities is not merely to deliver input for the sake of delivering it. Rather, learners are purposefully pushed to attend to particular forms in the input and make meaning-focused decisions. This pushing is ultimately realized via some type of language task that has a central objective: to accomplish something tangible. These goals may involve matching one concept with another, choosing among various ideas to find the one that corresponds, or selecting between drawings or photos. Still other SI activities might involve evaluating the truth value of a set of utterances. Again, variety within a set of activities is always recommended, but within this variety the common thread is always to have a task of some type that learners are to accomplish by attending to and making decisions about the SI that is presented orally or on the written page.

Activity D   My Summer Vacation

Listen carefully to each sentence your instructor reads about his or her upcoming vacation. Notice the use of *will* to denote future.

> INSTRUCTOR'S SCRIPT
> This summer, I will spend two weeks in Europe. When I get back, I will take a road trip with my family. I will work in a bookstore for the rest of the summer to earn some extra money. Then, I plan to get a head start on Fall classes.

Activity D lacks an apparent purpose. That is, this activity is designed to deliver input but never demands anything from the learner. Since there is nothing for the learner to do, this type of design functions more as a set of examples that might accompany a traditional grammatical explanation. Activity D contrasts sharply with an activity that forces L2 learners to notice and subsequently process the meaning of particular target features. For example, in affective Activity E, learners must attend to the meaning of the future tense forms in order to truly express their opinions and beliefs and thus complete the activity.

Activity E   My Summer Vacation: Two Different Perspectives

Step 1. Are teachers' lives really that different from their students'? Read about your instructor's plans for this summer and decide whether or not each activity would be fun for you.

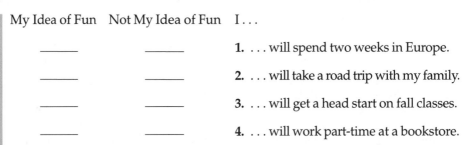

My Idea of Fun	Not My Idea of Fun	I . . .
———	———	**1.** . . . will spend two weeks in Europe.
———	———	**2.** . . . will take a road trip with my family.
———	———	**3.** . . . will get a head start on fall classes.
———	———	**4.** . . . will work part-time at a bookstore.

[more activity items of the same format]

Step 2. One of these statements made by the instructor is not true. Can you guess which activity your instructor is *not* actually planning? Together with a partner, see if you can agree on which one is false and be ready to announce your guess.

Finally, note the follow-up step that was included with Activity E. This gives the activity even more purpose. Not only will learners do something immediately with the input, but they will also need to report to their classmates on their responses to the items. Having a context for an activity and having learners do something with the input, both immediately and later in pairs or groups, goes a long way in motivating learners to attend to the content of each input string.

Pitfall #4: Not presenting both oral and written input.

This pitfall is both easy to understand and easy to remedy. In my experience as a language program director, FL instructors often tend to neglect giving oral input. Perhaps this is due to a desire for learners to see the forms and how they are spelled. The obvious problem with limiting learner exposure to the written mode alone is that, although they will be able to interpret (read) and produce (write) the target forms, learners will not be pushed to distinguish sounds that differentiate tense, aspect, mood, and other features of a given language. In turn, this may affect their ability to orally produce these sound sequences, since they have not made sound-meaning mappings (only written form-meaning mappings). For this reason, it is indispensable for instructors to include both types of input. Effective activity design is not easy—it takes a concerted effort on the part of the designer to ensure that learners get activity items that are (a) sufficient in quantity, (b) suitably varied in content and lexical items chosen, and (c) both oral and written in nature.

Pitfall #5: Not moving from sentences to connected discourse.

Activities that appear early in a lesson should require learners to process language only at the sentence level, not at the discourse level. That is, having learners process a paragraph of information or an entire dialogue or conversation is certainly not optimal during the early stages of their exposure to a particular structure. Attentional resources are quickly depleted, because learners exhaust their available capacity just grasping the overall meaning of a discourse. Discourse-level SI activities should appear later, after learners have begun noticing and processing the target form. Although instructors who are beginning SI activity design seem to struggle more with writing sentence-level activity items, discourse-level activities are still very important. Activity F is a good example of an SI activity that incorporates connected discourse.

Activity F   A Student's Weekend

Listen to the following story that a student told about his weekend and decide which statements accurately describe what happened.

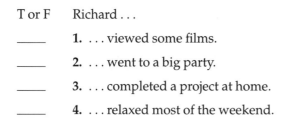

T or F   Richard . . .

_____   **1.** . . . viewed some films.

_____   **2.** . . . went to a big party.

_____   **3.** . . . completed a project at home.

_____   **4.** . . . relaxed most of the weekend.

> INSTRUCTOR'S SCRIPT
> My weekend was really relaxed. I just went out once to visit a friend at his apartment. Other than that, I stayed up late every night watching movies I rented and shopping for a new tennis racket on eBay. I finished all my homework on Friday, so I played around most of the weekend. I called my parents on Sunday just to check up on the new house they are building. All in all, it was a pretty low-key weekend.

Pitfall #6: Not keeping the learners' processing strategies in mind.

A few researchers have set out to replicate the early PI studies and have made errors in materials design by not fashioning activity items based on Principles 1 and 2 and their corresponding subprinciples. Having reviewed these principles in this book, you are in a position to avoid this pitfall fairly easily. The most obvious ways in which learners' processing strategies can be disregarded are as follows.

- leaving redundant lexical items in the input strings together with the target morphology
- leaving the target form in a sentence-medial position when it is possible to make it more salient in utterance-initial position
- maintaining SVO word order with most or all activity items when learners could benefit from being exposed to OVS or other variations

In this book, you have been exposed to a variety of SI activities that introduce a number of grammatical features in five different languages. Still, even with the examples provided here, an instructor will have to make a concerted effort to review Principles 1 and 2 and realize their implications for L2 structures not discussed herein. By not keeping the Lexical Preference Principle in mind, instructors eliminate incentives for students to attend to tense markers, aspect markers, mood markers, and so on. If one ignores the Sentence Location Principle during activity design, learners may not even notice the presence of a target form at all. Finally, if instructors disregard (or are not aware of) the fact that their students are relying on the First Noun Principle, they may delay or prevent the acquisition of certain features related to the subject-object relationship including word order, case markings, and object pronouns. An instructor must keep in mind what the learners are "doing" or what is happening in their heads if he or she expects the activities to promote more noticing and processing than raw, unstructured input would bring about. Otherwise, SI activities become input activities devoid of any specific psycholinguistic motivation.

Pitfall #7: Not attending to utterance length during activity design.

You may recall that learners are more likely to notice and subsequently process a form when other forms in a given utterance are processed at little or no cost to attentional resources. This fact has two immediate implications regarding writing items for an SI activity. First, instructors should take measures to ensure that utterances include only known vocabulary. If learners are struggling (and using up attentional resources) to even comprehend the overall meaning of an utterance, they are not likely to notice and process a particular target form that is the grammatical focus of a lesson. Conversely, if most or all words in a given utterance are processed easily by a learner, they will have leftover attentional resources to utilize for processing a novel form. Second, stimuli in SI activities should be short in length for a very similar reason. If, due to the quantity of words in an utterance, learners' attentional resources are exhausted, they are less likely to process a novel form in the input. For example, notice how long the utterances are in Activity G.

Activity G   The Model Student

Step 1. Do you consider yourself an organized, responsible student? Are you a sterling role model for others to follow? Let's find out! See how many characteristics of a responsible student match you.

A responsible student . . .

_____ **1.** . . . wakes up early to have a balanced breakfast before class.

_____ **2.** . . . lays out the clothes he or she is going to wear the night before.

_____ **3.** . . . arrives at school early to review for class discussions.

_____ **4.** . . . tries to get all his or her homework done before dinner.

_____ **5.** . . . goes to bed early so he or she can get eight hours of sleep.

_____ **6.** . . . falls asleep quickly and easily because he or she has worked so hard.

Step 2. Are any of the actions in Step 1 overly responsible, bordering on obsessive? Which ones? Be ready to share your thoughts.

Are all the words in each utterance necessary in order to convey the general meaning of each statement? Were you able to find ways in which the input strings could be shortened? Look at the alternative illustrated in Activity H.

The same main ideas are communicated in this activity, without overtaxing learners' attentional resources. In which activity (G or H) do you believe learners are more likely to process the present tense verb forms?

Activity H   The Model Student

Step 1. Do you consider yourself an organized, responsible student? Are you a sterling role model for others to follow? Let's find out! See how many characteristics match you.

A responsible student . . .

_____ **1.** . . . wakes up early.

_____ **2.** . . . eats breakfast.

_____ **3.** . . . arrives early to class.

_____ **4.** . . . finishes homework before class.

_____ **5.** . . . goes to bed early.

_____ **6.** . . . falls asleep quickly.

Step 2. Are any of the actions in Step 1 overly responsible, bordering on obsessive? Which ones? Be ready to share your thoughts.

Pause to consider...

how the utterances in the following activity might be shortened in order to raise the probability that the conditional forms will be processed.

Activity I   Winning the Lottery

If I won the lottery, I . . .

_____ **1.** . . . would give some money to deserving charities.

_____ **2.** . . . would buy something nice for my parents or my best friend.

_____ **3.** . . . would put all the money in the bank and let it earn interest.

_____ **4.** . . . would invest in some stocks or bonds.

_____ **5.** . . . would probably spend it all right away.

_____ **6.** . . . would not even look for a job since I wouldn't need one.

Pitfall #8: Feeling the need to "remain faithful" to the language.

Some argue that SI activities do not remain faithful to the language in that there is an "unnatural" rearranging of elements within the utterances or an uncharacteristic division of clauses or phrases in order to make certain features more salient. For example, in Chapter 2, we looked at SI activities for third person singular verbs in English. In those activities the subjects were separated from the rest of the utterance so that the present forms would be nonredundant and therefore more likely to be processed. An activity from Chapter 2 is reproduced here (Activity J) for our discussion.

Activity J   Pop Culture Icons

A recent article in a pop culture magazine summarized the lives and contributions of major figures in the rock'n'roll industry. Below are just a few excerpts from the article. For each excerpt, decide whether the author of the article was referring to Sarah McLachlan or to both Bono and the Edge.

	Sarah McLachlan	Bono and the Edge
1. . . . travels all over the world.	_____	_____
2. . . . play the guitar.	_____	_____
3. . . . sings before thousands.	_____	_____
4. . . . writes a lot of songs.	_____	_____
5. . . . make videos for MTV and VH1.	_____	_____
6. . . . raises money for charities.	_____	_____

In this activity, the subject is separated out and placed at the top. This allows the target forms to appear in utterance-initial position and eliminates the normally redundant nature of the *-s* verb ending.

Some might argue (see Collentine, 2002) that fashioning activity items in this manner is not "ecologically valid." That is, because L2 input is not presented in the same way in which it would be presented in a natural (nonclassroom) setting, SI of this type is therefore fabricated and too artificial. Hence, Collentine and others might suggest that the separating of clauses from their corresponding utterances not be done and that target forms should appear in classroom activities just as they appear in natural settings (embedded within utterances). One can see this, for example, in the sample activity items from Collentine's (1998) subjunctive materials. With these activity items, Collentine has indeed achieved a more "natural" (unstructured) presentation of L2 input. However, this begs the question: does a more natural approach to delivering input work better than delivering the "unnatural" SI to the L2 learner? To date, no study has investigated whether SI for the Spanish subjunctive or other grammatical points yields more beneficial effects than does unstructured or "natural" input. However, the results of various studies focused on SI and the Spanish subjunctive, when compared with the outcome of other approaches to teaching the Spanish subjunctive, suggest that SI may be the most effective approach to date. In addition, evidence for the efficacy of SI in bringing about SLA of various other structures is overwhelming, as we have seen throughout this book.

In response to Collentine's arguments concerning the artificial nature of certain SI activities, I wrote the following:

> As for ecological validity, Collentine's point is valid. However, the mere fact that we teach grammar and get learners to practice it is an artifact of the classroom. Hence, drilling is an artifact. PI is an artifact. They are all artifacts of how we perceive what the classroom should be . . . Thus what is one person's ecological validity may not be another's . . . So-called "fragmentation" may not only be desirable, but it may be necessary (due to principle P1f) and appropriate for the learner to begin the process of making form-meaning connections.
>
> (Farley, 2002, pp. 892–893)

The bottom line is that no approach to focus-on-form grammar instruction is a perfect reflection of what takes place in natural settings. We easily recognize that drills, organized listening practice, reading comprehension questions, and so on typically occur only in the classroom context. In this sense, SI is no different.

Pitfall #9: Developing ungrammatical input strings as potential answers.

We must remember that input is what essentially drives SLA. This means that learners will be "using" whatever language data is at their fingertips to make hypotheses and draw conclusions about the target language. When instructors design activities that contain ungrammatical input as potential answers, they are doing a disservice to the learners who read or listen to these activities. Traditionally, ungrammatical input has been included in multiple choice and matching type activities without a second thought. However, now that we understand more about how languages are learned (noticing, processing form-meaning connections, integration into the developing system, and so on), this understanding sheds new light on the disadvantages of exposing learners to "bad" input. Activity K is an example of an activity that contains ungrammatical items as choices. This activity introduces the theme of furniture shopping, and its grammatical focus is adjective agreement. The main objective is that students select the grammatically correct answer.

Activity K   Furniture Shopping with Kelly Osborne

Kelly is going shopping to begin furnishing her new contemporary apartment in Manhattan. Select the grammatically correct answer to complete the following sentences:

1. *La sala es de estilo moderno. Así que Kelly necesita comprar...*

    The living room is in modern style. For this reason, Kelly needs to buy . . .

    a. *un sofá blanco.*   a white sofa.

    b. *una sofá blanca.*

    c. *una sofá blanco.*

    d. *un sofá blanca.*

2. *También debe comprar...*

She should also buy . . .

  a. *una silla negro.*   a black chair.

  b. *un silla negro.*

  c. *una silla negra.*

  d. *un silla negra.*

An activity with this kind of structure is extremely problematic. First, notice that it is entirely mechanical in that learners can disregard the title, instruction line, and even the numbered items themselves. All the learner must do is select the one correct noun phrase that contains adjective agreement. In addition, three out of four options are grammatically incorrect. While this may seem like a good way to "test" the learner, in actual fact this is an example of extremely poor activity design. Remember that the goal is to *teach* the learner via these activities. Since we know that L2 learners acquire via input, we should not feed them any bad input. Instead of including input strings that are ungrammatical, an instructor can achieve the same goal and design a very similar activity while still limiting items to grammatical input. This is illustrated in the affective Activity L.

Activity L   Furniture Shopping with Kelly Osborne

Step 1. Kelly is going shopping to begin furnishing her new contemporary apartment in Manhattan. She loves the modern, even space-age, look. Which colors do you recommend she choose?

1. *un sofá...* (a sofa)
  a. *morado* (purple)
  b. *azul* (blue)
  c. *blanco* (white)
  d. *anaranjado* (orange)

2. *una silla ...* (a chair)
  a. *morada* (purple)
  b. *negra* (black)
  c. *verde* (green)
  d. *roja* (red)

3. *una mesa...* (a table)
  a. *metálica* (metallic)
  b. *amarilla* (yellow)
  c. *azul* (blue)
  d. *blanca* (white)

4. *una alfombra...* (a rug)
  a. *roja y verde* (red and green)
  b. *blanca y negra* (black and white)
  c. *blanca y roja* (white and red)
  d. *negra y roja* (black and red)

Step 2. Compare your answers with a partner. Did you both agree on how to decorate Kelly's contemporary apartment?

Pitfall #10: Creating "giveaway" items through poor vocabulary choice.

Sometimes instructors fail to play the role of the student after designing an activity. That is, they neglect to carry out the activity themselves as if they were language learners. Inevitably, revisions will be needed even for the most experienced activity designer, and perhaps the most typical mistake made with regard to content is the inclusion of "giveaway" vocabulary. This type of pitfall is illustrated in Activity M.

Activity M   Why Are They Famous?

Match the famous person to the activity they are best known for:

_____ has played basketball for the Los Angeles Lakers and the Miami Heat.   **a.** Julia Child

_____ has lived in the White House.   **b.** Shaquille O'Neal

_____ has written many gourmet cookbooks.   **c.** David Letterman

_____ has written horror books such as *Carrie* and *Misery*.   **d.** the President

_____ has appeared on *Late Night* for years.   **e.** Stephen King

Notice that in Activity M it is possible to answer many of the activity items without even reading or fully understanding the utterances. Note that this type of oversight also often occurs in the design of listening comprehension and reading comprehension passages. Instructors often reveal the correct answer through including proper nouns (names of famous people, famous places, and so on) that essentially make comprehending the target language irrelevant to arriving at the logical response to comprehension questions.

Pause to consider . . .

how you could rewrite Activity M to avoid the lexical giveaways. Go back and look over each item in Activity M and think about how to describe each famous person without using proper nouns. Can you make learners attend to the verb forms themselves?

PART 2: FREQUENTLY ASKED QUESTIONS

The second half of this chapter addresses common questions and concerns related to the use of SI activities in the L2 classroom.

FAQ #1: What if students grow tired of the same basic format for SI activities?

There is nothing like a lack of variety in activity design to cause students to get bored with an instructor's lesson plan. It is important for every instructor to realize that students will exhibit a variety of learning preferences. With regard to SI activities, some students may prefer seeing the target forms, whereas others will want to hear them, and still others will need both written and aural input before they are able to adequately attend to and process a given structure.

Instructors should also take special care in varying the format of the SI activities delivered during one class hour. One activity might be true/false, whereas another might involve matching. One might be multiple-choice involving utterance selection; another might use photos, drawings, or other types of visual stimuli. In addition, remember that SI activities will not normally appear alone during a class hour. That is, they will most likely be accompanied by output-centered activities as well as activities of a totally different nature such as reading comprehension activities, listening comprehension passages, and activities focused on culture.

In addition, sometimes instructors demonstrate through the design of their lesson plans an unbalanced preference (almost an obsession) for teaching grammar to the exclusion of other aspects of the target language. This lack of equilibrium in presenting the L2 and its culture(s) inevitably leads to boredom in the classroom. In general, L2 learners are most concerned with grasping meaning, "getting the gist," and learning about interesting content. An instructor who spends an inordinate amount of time on grammar alone inevitably is forced into using an overabundance of SI activities or some other approach to focus on form, driving students to boredom. Although this book has focused exclusively on the design of SI activities, it is essential to note that these are only a few among many types of activities that are regularly designed and presented in a healthy, stimulating L2 classroom atmosphere.

FAQ #2: What then is the role of output (production) practice?

As Lee and VanPatten (1995, 2003) point out, the role of output practice is to promote fluency and accuracy. Whereas SI activities interact with the processes involved when the L2 is entering learners' developing systems, structured output activities provide contexts for the processes related to access and production to be perfected with regard to both speed and precision.

Numerous SLA studies have shown processing instruction (SI + EI) to be more effective than output practice alone in bringing about improvement on interpretation tasks as well as oral and written production tasks. With publication and widespread citation naturally came some misunderstandings and misconceptions regarding the conclusions reached in these studies. One common misconception has been to presume that those who conducted early PI research might advocate an SI-only approach to grammar instruction. Nothing could be farther from the truth, as evidenced in Lee and VanPatten (1995, 2003) and some of the articles published (see, for example, Farley 2001a). Although all contemporary theoretical frameworks of SLA ascribe a principal role to input, there is no framework that excludes output practice as a beneficial and/or necessary part of SLA. The Input Processing framework (see VanPatten, 1996) is no exception. Although it focuses on L2 learner strategies that occur during on-line processing of input, the framework should be seen as complimentary to (rather than opposed to) frameworks that outline production processes—Pienemann's (1998) Processability Theory, for example, among others.

FAQ #3: Which is better, referential or affective SI activities?

"Better" is not the most accurate term to use when differentiating between referential and affective SI activities. These two types of activities should be seen as having different functions; for that reason, they cannot be measured on the same scale of worth or value to the learner. The principal benefit of referential activities is that they force learners to attend to the target form. Simply put, if learners do not attend to the form, they cannot consistently answer items correctly. The decisions required to complete referential activity items are always form- and meaning-based, but this is not the case with affective activities. With the latter, learners are merely asked to respond to L2 stimuli by expressing their opinions, feelings, or beliefs. This means that it will always be the meaning of each item (rather than the form and meaning) that will motivate learners' responses. If affective activities do not force learners to attend to form, why do they even exist within the Processing Instruction approach? The principal bene-fit of affective activities is that they allow learners to see the target forms in meaningful contexts and relate the meaning of each form to their own lives in some way. This function cannot be underestimated in maintaining the level of interest that learners have in a given lesson. Although level of interest and other affective measures are difficult (if not impossible) to accurately quantify, it is quite intuitive to hold that learners who care about the topic of a given activity and/or can relate to it personally in some way are more likely to pay attention to the utterances contained in the activity. Finally, although there is more than one right answer for affective activity items, they still provide a healthy dose of SI with the target feature in the most salient position.

FAQ #4: What should be the ratio and ordering of referential to affective activities?

Because referential activities push learners to pay attention to form and make decisions that are either right or wrong, it is ideal for them to precede affective activities whenever possible in a given class hour. Additionally, it is recom-mended that, for every affective SI activity, one to two referential activities be administered. In this way, learners become aware of the form via the referential activities first. Once "enlightened," they are more likely to continue to notice target forms during the affective activities in which noticing form (verb end-ings, for example) is not essential to successful completion. Of course, noticing does not by any means guarantee subsequent processing. However, with refer-ential activities coercing form-meaning mappings first, the effects of the affec-tive activities that follow are likely heightened and processing becomes more likely to occur.

FAQ #5: Which is better for the student, oral or written SI activities?

Although both types of activities are important, SI in the aural mode tends to be more often neglected in the L2 classroom. Instructors in general forget about the importance of the act of listening and the need that learners have to be able to distinguish L2 sounds and comprehend their distinct meanings. Presenting both written and aural SI to L2 learners is particularly important for languages in which orthography does not intuitively represent the sound system. Discerning the difference between first person and third person forms on paper, for example, is quite different from distinguishing how these forms sound dur-ing spontaneous oral production.

FAQ #6: How can I maintain a high level of creativity and keep students (even high school students) interested in my SI activities?

There is nothing like collaboration with other instructors to keep activities cre-ative and interesting. The old saying "two heads are better than one" certainly holds true when it comes to activity design. Without collaboration, instructors usually resort to focusing activities on themes with which they are very familiar—famous people they know, well-known places that they have visited, and so on. With two instructors contributing to the topics, subtopics, and the format(s) of an activity, the possibilities double; with three, they triple, and so on. As you partner with another instructor, consider brainstorming together regarding various categories of everyday life. The following are some suggested themes and subtopics.

Famous people

Politicians	Musicians
Actors and actresses	Artists
TV personalities	

Places

Cities or towns near the school	Students' hometowns
Local hotspots	Sites of current events
Vacation destinations	Places associated with well-known people

Activities

Daily routine activities	Seasonal activities
Weekend activities	Holiday fun

Experiences

Best and worst trips	This Happened to Me: True or False
Best and worst eating experiences	First dates
Most embarrassing moments	

Again, these are just a few ideas that will help get you started with brainstorming. Using these categories and subcategories as a starting point, a group of instructors can usually envision dozens of potential activities. Of course, certain ideas naturally intersect well with some grammatical points better than they do with others. Likewise, some fit well with a given chapter in your language textbook, and others do not. This is where logic, common sense, and discernment on the part of the instructor come into play. Keep in mind that the instructor is the one who must help learners transition from one activity to the next, so it is important that, for example, a transition from a book activity to a supplementary activity and back to another book activity be made smoothly.

A cautionary note concerning topic generation: be sensitive to your group of learners. Take, for instance, the topic of First Date. This topic may be entirely inappropriate for some groups, especially younger groups. Even more, some learners may have never been on a date, and this topic might put them in an awkward position. In general, there are two solutions to this issue: (1) avoid the potentially uncomfortable topic altogether, or (2) give students options that allow them to share with classmates one among *several* subtopics during a follow-up stage. Instead of sharing information about their first girlfriend or boyfriend, they might share about their best friend from high school, or their favorite high school teacher, or some other significant person from their past. Leaving an activity open-ended whenever possible is a sure way to avoid disaster, particularly when it comes to activities about friends, family, and other personal yet interesting life issues.

One principal objective in activity design is, of course, to appeal to your audience. This means getting to know them, their likes and dislikes, and their hobbies and interests. For this reason, it is a good idea to survey your students near the beginning of a semester or school year. In this way you will have a better idea of topics of interest and topics to avoid altogether. Keep in mind that interests among students come and go with time. For example, the sport of skateboarding was quite popular in the 70s through the mid-80s, yet it seemed to dwindle in popularity in the 90s. Only in the last few years with the broadcasting of the X-Games on ESPN and other media hype has it regained much of its popularity. Instructors must keep up with which topics are current and which are out of date. Trends come and go, and for that reason, activity topics should change with the times.

More importantly, instructors should be sensitive to *their* group of learners in particular. For instance, although skateboarding, snowboarding, and wakeboarding are all fairly popular right now, it may be that very few or none of the learners in your course participate in any of those activities. Keeping an eye on trends is important, but keeping an eye on your particular students' interests is crucial. Because of a simple lack of enthusiasm for a topic, learners may not pay attention to the L2 input in a given SI activity. If these learners will not attend to meaning (out of boredom), how can we expect them to notice and process form?

FAQ #7: This book has focused entirely on structured input. Aren't there other types of effective grammar instruction?

There are many approaches to L2 grammar instruction, including input flood, textual enhancement, and giving EI and/or corrective feedback. These are just some of the more prevalent approaches to focus on form that have been proposed in SLA literature in recent years.

The input flood approach (see Ellis, 1997) is based on the assumption that frequency of appearance in the input is a strong determiner of whether a form is acquired. Therefore, instructors who adhere to the input flood approach simply expose learners to numerous utterances (both written and aural) in which the target form is present in order to increase the likelihood that L2 input is taken (as intake) into learners' developing systems. Of course, one shortcoming of this approach is that the input is raw or unstructured in nature, so it is not purposely fashioned to keep the learners' input processing strategies in mind.

Textual enhancement is an approach that involves changing the appearance of written forms so that they are perceptually more salient. Changing font type and/or size, underlining the target forms, bolding them, coloring them, or placing them in italics are some ways that text might be enhanced. The idea is that, if learners are able to notice (perceive with the human eye) the forms more easily, they will subsequently be more likely to process them. There are numerous studies on the effects of textual enhancement, and not all agree on the effects of this approach (see, for example, Simard and Wong, 2001).

Giving EI and corrective feedback are approaches that do not normally stand alone. That is, these measures usually accompany some other approach to focus on form. For example, one might pair SI activities with certain types of

EI (see VanPatten, 1996) and/or corrective feedback (see Sanz & Morgan-Short, 2004). Explicit information, for many, simply means explaining how to form a particular structure, what that structure means, and when a structure can be used. Notice that all of this information is production-focused, helping learners to *produce* the correct form at the correct time in the correct location. However, as we have seen in this book, EI given to learners does not have to stop there. Learners can also be told why a particular form is difficult to notice and process; they can be informed of their own tendencies or processing strategies that function as hindrances during on-line comprehension. Whereas this EI is usually provided *before* learners begin processing practice, corrective feedback is given after learners have made "errors" in their output. This feedback can be explicit or implicit in nature, and, again, the value of corrective feedback is a debated issue in contemporary SLA literature (see, for example, Sanz and Morgan-Short, 2004, and Lightbown and Spada, 1999).

There are a number of approaches to grammar instruction, and some may work better than others in particular instances. It remains to be seen, for example, to what degree variables such as learning style, age, time allotted to instruction, and proficiency level affect the efficacy of these and other approaches to focus on form. Despite the need for further investigation into instruction types in general, at present, SI stands alone as the most rigorously investigated type of instructional intervention with regard to variety of languages and grammar points examined.

FAQ #8: I have heard that this input-focused approach (SI) does not promote accuracy and that if I want my students to be accurate with the language, this approach is not the best. Is that true?

Although this argument seems to be raised fairly often, it really makes no sense given the nature of the research carried out on SI. All the assessment tasks in the published research to date on SI have always taken into account accuracy when determining scores for each participant. That is, when pre-test scores on a written or an oral production task were compared with corresponding post-test scores, statistical analyses were carried out with regard to accuracy. If forms were not correctly produced in those tasks, without fail either half or full credit (depending on the study) was deducted from a participant's score. To claim that SI brings about fluency but not accuracy is entirely unfounded. In fact, it would be more precise to say the opposite, since SI studies have taken into account accuracy but have not been designed to assess fluency. Those who pose such an argument are merely speculating or voicing their opinion based on what they think might be happening with SI. The extensive research on SI, however, reveals effects that one might not intuitively guess—that SI consistently brings about improvement with regard to accuracy on both written and oral production tasks.

FAQ #9: How compatible are SI activities with technology? Have they been successfully integrated into online curriculums?

Computer-assisted language learning in general has recently added a new dimension with the development of interactive course management programs. Numerous programs now provide a secure web platform to deliver, evaluate, and grade student activities. Electronic workbook formats (using Blackboard, WebCT, or similar platforms) for SI activities enable instructors to supplement or replace traditionally mediated activities (paper/pen, instructor's script, and so on) with state-of-the-art SI activities that integrate audio, images, and text. The SI format in particular works well with an internet-delivered workbook format, because responses to activity items are usually short (especially with true/false, matching, and multiple choice) and easily evaluated. Because SI activities usually have a very limited number of possible answers, feedback is easily programmed into online SI workbooks as well.

One example of implementing a web-based platform for the delivery of SI activities is at University of Notre Dame. Here, I introduced low-level Spanish learners to a WebCT-based workbook (adapted from Feustle, 2001) containing SI activities that corresponded with chapter themes from the textbook *¿Sabías que...?* (VanPatten et al., 2000). In the next chapter, I present student surveys conducted after one semester and four semesters of implementation. The survey results indicate a remarkable ease of use and a rapid decrease in technical difficulties after learners' first use of the workbook. Student response regarding educational content was promising, with over 70% of students rating the educational value of the activities as "good" to "excellent."

Of course, I am not the only researcher who has implemented web-based workbooks in order to deliver SI activities. Cristina Sanz at Georgetown University, Diane Musumeci at the University of Illinois at Urbana-Champaign, and others have also utilized Blackboard and other web-based platforms for activity delivery with similar success. In addition, McGraw-Hill has published an electronic Quia workbook to accompany *¿Sabías que...?* that contains some SI activities. More details on my own implementation of a web-based SI workbook at Notre Dame are included in the final chapter of this book.

FAQ #10: Is the nature of a grammar point a significant factor in student learning?

As an instruction type, SI has been shown to be effective with many types of L2 features including past tense, present progressive, future tense, subjunctive mood, and object pronouns. In the next chapter, we will look at some research indicating that SI brought about learning in individuals who were theoretically "unready" to learn a particular feature. In closing, while the nature of a grammatical point does play some role in learning, SI has been shown to work with both "simple" and "complex" target features.

READ MORE ABOUT IT

Farley, A. P. (2002). Processing instruction, communicative value, and ecological validity: A response to Collentine's defense. *Hispania* 85: 889–895.

Lee, J., & VanPatten, B. (2003). *Making communicative language teaching happen* (2d ed.). New York: McGraw-Hill.

VanPatten, B., ed. (2004). *Processing instruction: Theory, research, and commentary.* Mahwah, NJ: Erlbaum.

CHAPTER 6

New Research on SI

INTRODUCTION

In this chapter, I introduce some new research related to SI and its importance to L2 learners. Here, we take a closer look at the design, implementation, and results of two studies. The first study we review is a research experiment that focuses on low-level learners. Are these learners truly limited in what they can be taught, or can SI enable them to notice and process language structures typically reserved for more proficient learners? The results challenge some prevalent theoretical notions that suggest learners should not be taught certain structures until they are "ready" to learn them. The results also suggest that learner difficulties with certain structures may lie more with the manner in which they are presented than with the nature of the structures themselves.

The second study contained in this chapter presents learner feedback on SI activities, in this case SI activities that were presented as an online workbook. The use of electronic media is rapidly expanding throughout the educational community as teachers perceive the advantages of computer-based tools. However, before jumping on any bandwagon we must assess whether it is possible to effectively integrate the SI approach with new technologies. This study examines the implementation of a new Web-based workbook of SI activities to complement a university-level Spanish curriculum.

STUDY 1: FARLEY AND MCCOLLAM WIEBE STRUCTURED INPUT—TEACHING THE UNLEARNABLE?

Developmental Stages

Over the past few decades, SLA research has indicated that L2 learners tend to pass through certain stages of development as they acquire the L2. Whether they learn the language during time spent abroad or in the foreign language classroom, all learners tend to acquire the same language features in the same order.

Groundbreaking ESL studies over thirty years ago first identified these developmental sequences in learners. This research is now supported by studies of many other languages including German, Japanese, Swedish, and Spanish. Research to date also suggests that instruction has been ineffective in altering the order in which learners progress through these stages. Introducing language structures that learners are not ready for has so far proven to be of little benefit.

One of the theoretical frameworks that has attempted to explain why learners pass through these stages and why learner progression does not appear to be affected by instruction is called Processability Theory. This framework, first proposed in Pienemann (1998), suggests that humans have an unconscious apparatus for creating speech. In order to produce in an L2, a learner first needs to acquire specific procedures. Pienemann proposed a specific development sequence for five basic production procedures that he claims exist (Table 6.1). He suggested that all learners, regardless of learning or instructional style, acquire these procedures independently and in the specific order given. Using this sequence, it should therefore be possible to predict which language structures learners will acquire first and which will be delayed until the corresponding procedure is developed. Table 6.1 lists the five procedures proposed by Pienemann together with some target language structures that should be produced after each procedure is acquired.

Pienemann's hierarchy of production procedures can be easily understood when one looks at L2 features in terms of memory constraints during real-time speech production and distance within an utterance. There are "local" features and "long distance" features. That is, Pienemann's hierarchy starts with production at the word level, then moves to stages involving the phrase level, and ends with the clause level. To be aware that particular forms need to be produced, a learner must be able to transfer semantic information across certain boundaries: word boundaries, phrase boundaries, and clause boundaries. You can intuitively understand how it would be easy to transfer information over a shorter distance; transferring information a longer distance would be more difficult. This is precisely the reasoning behind Pienemann's hierarchy.

Pienemann's proposed stages have given rise to the concept of learner readiness. Have certain L2 learners reached the stage where they can produce a certain language feature? Or are they "unready," still needing to develop production procedures that they do not yet possess? These are the types of research

TABLE 6.1 Pienemann's (1998) Hierarchy of Processing Procedures

Processing procedures	Structural outcome	Example (Spanish)
5. Subordinate clause procedure	main and subordinate clause	subjunctive
4. S-procedure	interphrasal information exchange	subject-verb agreement
3. Phrasal procedure	phrasal information exchange	noun phrase agreement
2. Category procedure	lexical morphemes	past tense marking
1. Word / lemma access	"words"	single word

questions that have sprung from the theoretical notion of readiness. Studies investigating readiness have found mixed results. Testing "ready" and "unready" learners to see whether they benefited equally from instruction has shown that in some cases, ready learners benefit while unready learners are unaffected. In other cases, all learners—whether ready or unready—improved at the same rate.

Relevant to the present study is the fact that production of the personal *a* case marker in Spanish involves an information transfer across the phrase boundary, whereas use of the subjunctive involves the longer distance exchange of information across a clause boundary. Within the five stages, Pienemann places structures such as personal *a* at stage three, whereas the subjunctive appears in the final stage. Pienemann's colleague, Johnston (1995), applied Processability Theory to Spanish and developed *seven* stages rather than five. Still, Johnston also placed personal *a* near the middle of his hierarchy (stage five) and the subjunctive at the top (stage seven). This discussion of Processability Theory and the Pienemann and Johnston hierarchies has been purposely brief. What you should understand is that both Pienemann and Johnston predict that intermediate L2 learners of Spanish who are "ready" for personal *a* (but do not yet produce it) are definitely "unready" for the subjunctive. The purpose of Farley and McCollam Wiebe's study was to test the validity of this claim.

Teaching the Unlearnable

Throughout this book, we have seen how SI can bring about improvement on a number of language tasks including written interpretation tasks, written production tasks, and oral production tasks. Research has also shown that this improvement is greater than that observed when other types of instruction are used that do not take into account the processing strategies of the learner. Pienemann and Johnston would hold that, whether you introduce learners to SI or any other type of instruction, it should not make a difference if learners are not "ready."

The reason why this study is so important is that none of the studies investigating learner readiness thus far have used SI or processing instruction (SI + EI) as instruction types. Can SI make a difference? If unready learners demonstrate improvement after receiving SI instruction, then this instruction type has altered not only the *rate* but also the *order* of L2 acquisition. This finding would challenge the widely accepted concept of stages of development (at least the stages articulated by Pienemann and Johnston).

Farley and McCollam Wiebe (2005) asked the question: will learners be able to produce a given form only if they are ready for it, or will the way in which the target form is presented to them determine whether they can produce it or not? We selected two grammatical structures to present to low- to mid-intermediate Spanish learners: the personal *a* object marker and the subjunctive mood. You probably recall that we looked at SI for object pronouns in Spanish in Chapter 4, and SI for the Spanish subjunctive in Chapter 3 of this book. Personal *a* belongs to the stage that our intermediate learners would naturally acquire next (stage five in Johnston's scheme), and therefore instruction—any type of instruction—should assist in acquisition. In contrast, both Johnston and Pienemann label the Spanish subjunctive as a final-stage form. According to them, low- to mid-intermediate learners should *not* be ready for this form. Using a final-stage form allowed us to examine whether learners could benefit from instruction for which Pienemann and Johnston would say they were not ready.

Experimental Design

For this study, we chose as subjects Spanish students from the University of Illinois who were enrolled in intermediate Spanish courses. Through written surveys and oral interviews, we eliminated any students whose native language was not English or who were proficient in other languages. We also eliminated any participants who had received previous instruction on these two forms, as well as those who produced forms that suggested they might have already reached Johnston's final stage. In this way we ensured that all participants would be presented with features that they had not yet acquired—one for which they were "ready" (personal *a*) and one for which they were "unready" (subjunctive). After eliminations, we were left with twenty-nine participants. We then divided them into four different groups in order to evaluate the effects of instruction type. The first group received full processing instruction (PI group), which includes both SI and EI about the language feature. The second group received SI only (SI group), without any EI. The third group received only EI (EI group), and the fourth was a control group (C group) that received no instruction at all.

Instructional Materials

Instruction for the PI group and the SI group was carried out using SI activities with personal *a* and the subjunctive in focus. For each form, we presented the students with four aural SI activities and six written SI activities. Two affective activities and three referential activities, two of which were aural and three of which were written, were administered on each of the two days of instruction. Instruction for each structure was administered over two consecutive classes that lasted 50 minutes each, for a total of 100 minutes of exposure to the treatment.

Activities A–D are examples of the referential and affective activity items we used to present each form. After completing the activity, the students were told the correct answer but were never given an explanation for why those answers were correct. It is important to note that the SI activities never required the students to produce any of the target forms, neither personal *a* nor the subjunctive.

Activity A   Referential SI Activity Items: Object Marker a

Select the best rendition of each sentence.

> **1.** *A mi mamá la besa mucho mi papá.*
> > **a.** My mom kisses my dad a lot.
> > **b.** My dad kisses my mom a lot.
>
> **2.** *A mi papá no lo comprendo yo.*
> > **a.** I don't understand my dad.
> > **b.** My dad doesn't understand me.

(Farley & McCollam Wiebe, 2005)

In designing the SI activities for personal *a,* we specifically accounted for P1e and Principle 2. In Chapter 1, we discussed these principles and saw how a learner will process only less meaningful forms (such as personal *a*) when their attentional resources are not overburdened. For this reason, we specifically used short SI activity items in the instructional materials that contained familiar vocabulary. You may also recall from Chapter 4 that Principle 2 tells us that the learner will automatically assume the first noun in an utterance is the subject, unless context or other lexical semantic clues suggest otherwise. Since sentences with personal *a* frequently use SVO order, learners can often decipher who is doing what to whom without paying attention to personal *a.* To combat the ability of learners to ignore the object marker, we deliberately included many utterances with OVS word order so that the FNP would fail them during their interpretation practice.

Activity B   Affective SI Activity Items: Object Marker a

As the largest generation of American citizens ages, our society is becoming older, with senior citizens outnumbering other age groups. How do you think the older generation feels about the younger generations? And how do young people feel about those much older? Mark the following statements **Cierto** or **Falso** according to your personal opinion.

Cierto	Falso	*A la Generación X no la comprenden los viejos.*
		Older people don't understand Generation X.
Cierto	Falso	*A los viejos no los respetan los jóvenes.*
		Young people don't respect their elders.

(Farley & McCollam Wiebe, 2005)

In designing SI for the subjunctive, we kept in mind Principle 1 and P1f, the Sentence Location Principle. Remember that subjunctives are difficult to process, because they generally occur in sentence-medial position where forms are least likely to be noticed. In order to make the subjunctives more salient, the main clause was separated from the subordinate clause in each activity. As you may remember from Chapter 3, this accomplishes two things. First, it places subjunctives in utterance-initial position. Second, it eliminates the redundancy that normally occurs when both the main clause and the subjunctive express uncertainty.

Activity C   Referential SI Activity Items: The Subjunctive

Based on what your instructor says, place a check by the phrase that best completes each statement.

INSTRUCTOR'S SCRIPT	Complete the statement.
1. *Es cierto que muchos atletas profesionales...* It's true that many professional athletes . . .	**1.** _____ *comen comida muy sana.* _____ *coman comida muy sana.* eat healthy food.

<table>
<tr><td>
INSTRUCTOR'S SCRIPT (CONTINUED)

2. *No creo que los Rolling Stones...*
I don't believe the Rolling Stones . . .

3. *No es probable que todos los actores...*
It's not probable that all actors . . .
</td></tr>
</table>

2. _____ *cantan muy bien.*

_____ *canten muy bien.*

sing very well.

3. _____ *son muy arrogantes.*

_____ *sean muy arrogantes.*

are very arrogant.

(Farley & McCollam Wiebe, 2005)

The PI group received EI in addition to the SI activities, whereas the EI group received EI only. For both language forms, the EI was written in English to ensure learner comprehension, with examples provided in Spanish. The EI regarding personal *a* discussed how the marker is used to identify the object of an utterance. It explained that Spanish allows for word orders other than SVO and that the first noun in an utterance is not always the subject. The EI for the subjunctive instructed the students regarding the meaning and the use of the subjunctive form. It provided examples of subjunctive forms and discussed where the subjunctive is located. The students were warned of the subjunctive's redundancy. The EI about the subjunctive only addressed its use in subordinate clauses after expressions of uncertainty.

Activity D   Affective Activity Items: The Subjunctive

Give your opinion about each statement. Is it referring to Homer and Bart or Marge and Lisa Simpson? Perhaps some of the statements describe all of them. Maybe others don't describe any of them.

No es muy probable que...	Homer y Bart	Marge y Lisa
It's not very probable that . . .		
les guste la música clásica. they like classical music.	_____	_____
digan la verdad siempre. they tell the truth always.	_____	_____
sean perezosos/as. they are lazy.	_____	_____
eviten sus responsabilidades. they avoid their responsibilities.	_____	_____

(Farley & McCollam Wiebe, 2005)

Assessing Learner Performance Before and After Instruction

The experiment was carried out in three sessions. During the first session, students completed a background questionnaire and two pre-tests: a grammaticality judgment task (GJT) and picture description task (PDT). The purpose of the grammaticality judgment test (GJT) was to assess the students' underlying knowledge of personal *a* and the subjunctive and to eliminate students who already knew these forms. As shown in Box A, participants were asked to read written sentences in Spanish and responded by marking (a) possible, (b) not possible, or (c) I don't know. They were also asked to correct any utterances that they had marked as "not possible." The reason they were asked to correct utterances is because we wanted to know whether the learners had marked a given utterance as "not possible" for the right reason.

BOX A. Grammaticality judgment test instruction line and sample assessment items

<u>Instructions:</u> Read the following Spanish sentences and indicate whether each is **Possible** or **Not Possible** by circling your choice, or select the **I Don't Know** option if you don't know. If you indicate that a sentence is **Not Possible,** write in the necessary correction that would make the sentence possible.

1. *Es imposible que Juan venga antes.* (Possible) Not Possible I Don't Know

2. *No hay estudiantes de filosofía en mi residencia.* Possible Not Possible (I Don't Know)

3. *La abogada defiende a su cliente.* Possible (Not Possible) I Don't Know

---

To evaluate students' ability to produce the target forms, we used a picture description task (PDT). The pictures were specifically designed to bring forth production of personal *a* and the subjunctive if indeed the learners were capable of doing so. For example, the PDT for personal *a* asked students to describe pictures that showed a cat biting his owner (a context where the object marker would be obligatory), a picture of a girl playing the piano (a context where an object marker would not be obligatory), or a picture of people walking around in a downtown area (a distracter item where personal *a* should not be produced). For the subjunctive, the PDT showed the students a picture with two phrases printed above the picture. Students were asked to give their opinion about the scene by choosing one of the two main clauses provided and completing the utterance. This PDT presented pictures and phrases designed to cause the student to produce subjunctive and nonsubjunctive (indicative) tokens, as well as distracter items. For example, participants would see an image of a dog playing the guitar along with the phrases *Es cierto que...* (It is true that . . .) and *Es dudoso que...* (It is doubtful that . . .) provided above the picture. A distracter item would show a person in the kitchen cooking eggs along with the expressions: *Es difícil...* (It is difficult . . .) and *No es difícil...* (It is not difficult . . .).

Participants completed the PDT in a one-on-one session with one of the researchers, and it was audio recorded. After the pre-test, we analyzed the recording to determine at what stage of development each of the twenty-nine learners was beginning. His or her beginning stage was then used to classify each student as either ready or unready for personal *a* and/or the subjunctive. In the second session, students received instruction on the object marker, following which GJT and PDT post-tests were administered. Finally, in the third session, students received instruction on the subjunctive, and the same type of post-test was administered to assess their performance on this form. For the pre-test, both target forms (*a* and subjunctive) were included on the GJT and PDT, along with distracter items. For the post-tests, however, the GJT and PDT evaluated student performance only on the language form that had just been presented.

We scored learners' responses to target items on the GJT as correct or incorrect by comparing them to native speaker judgments for the same sentences. For the PDT, we calculated an emergence score and an accuracy score. The emergence score indicated whether the student produced the target form during the PDT and was used to assess the developmental stage of the student. We used the accuracy score to determine whether any instruction type brought about effects that were significantly different from the other treatments. Accuracy was scored using a ratio of correct uses to obligatory contexts. For example, if a learner produced six utterances that required personal *a* but used the marker only three times in those six utterances, then that learner was given an accuracy ratio of 3/6, or 0.5.

Results

Did the learners who were classified as "unready" for a feature show any improvement after instruction? Did SI activities bring about any beneficial effects? According to the PDT data, almost all the twenty-nine learners were categorized as ready for the object marker *a*, which meant that they should be capable of producing this form after treatment. However, fewer than half of those students who were classified as "ready" actually showed development in producing personal *a* following instruction. None of the participants in this study were categorized as ready for the subjunctive. However, all the students who received PI (SI + EI) showed development following instruction, and nearly half of the other learners (with the exception of the C group) also showed subjunctive development.

For accuracy on the PDT, we found that both readiness and instruction had a significant effect. Strangely, we found that ready learners were *less* accurate than unready learners. As before, all three treatments brought about results significantly different from the C group. However, this time there was no significant difference between any instruction types. Accuracy improved with all three types of instruction, and it did not seem to matter which type of instruction they received. A summary of all results is provided in Table 6.2 and Figure 6.1.

For the GJT, we found a significant effect (negative) for learner readiness, no effect for instruction type, and no significant interaction between readiness and instruction type. For emergence of the language forms on the PDT (i.e., whether the learner was capable of producing the form at all), the results yielded no significant effect for learner readiness. Whether or not a learner was able to produce the form following instruction did not seem to depend at all on how the learner had been classified (ready or unready). There was a significant effect for instruction with all three types—EI group, SI group, and PI group—having significantly higher scores than the C group. This means that instruction did play a significant role in determining whether or not the

TABLE 6.2 Frequencies of Development by Treatment Group and Structure (Farley & McCollam Wiebe, 2005)

Structure	Treatment	No. of ready learners	Showed development
Object marker	EI	6	2
	SI	7	2
	PI	6	3
	Control	6	0
Subjunctive	EI	0	2
	SI	0	3
	PI	0	6
	Control	0	0

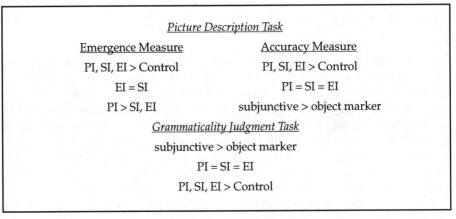

> *Picture Description Task*
>
> Emergence Measure   Accuracy Measure
>
> PI, SI, EI > Control   PI, SI, EI > Control
>
> EI = SI   PI = SI = EI
>
> PI > SI, EI   subjunctive > object marker
>
> *Grammaticality Judgment Task*
>
> subjunctive > object marker
>
> PI = SI = EI
>
> PI, SI, EI > Control

FIGURE 6.1 Summary of All Results (Farley & McCollam Wiebe, 2005)

learner could produce the form. PI brought about significantly more improvement than did EI and SI; however, no statistical difference was found between EI and SI.

Conclusions

Whether or not the learners were classified as "ready" to learn a form had no effect on whether they actually were able to produce it. Instruction did have a significant positive effect on emergence and accuracy. Following instruction, unready learners were able to produce the form just like ready learners. In terms of accuracy, unready learners actually produced the form more accurately than did ready learners following instruction. PI (SI +EI) brought about the greatest improvement, followed by SI and EI. Regarding accuracy, all three treatment types appear to have brought about equal improvements.

Recall that Pienemann and Johnston hold that instruction under no circumstances results in a learner producing a form for which they have not yet developed the corresponding procedures. The results of our study suggest that, rather than tailoring a curriculum to what is perceived to be learners' current or next stage, carefully structuring the input (SI) and warning learners about processing strategies that may fail them (EI) can result in the emergence of so-called "late-stage" forms.

STUDY 2: FARLEY
LEARNER REACTIONS TO SI ACTIVITIES ON-LINE

You have already read about some of the research that indicates the effectiveness of SI activities, yet we rarely have a chance to ask students themselves how they feel certain activities have contributed to their learning experience. The second half of this chapter will present the results of a student survey following implementation of an electronic SI activity workbook for beginning Spanish learners at the University of Notre Dame.

Introduction

The past decade has witnessed exponential growth in computer use in higher education. In the early 1990s, student email accounts, 24-hour computer laboratories, and universitywide Ethernet connections were the domain of computer science and engineering programs. Now, such amenities are standard for students of all disciplines at most institutes of tertiary education across the United States. Given the widespread availability of computer-related technology and the increasing familiarity of students with this technology, it is only logical that we harness this potential to enhance language-learning programs.

Technology has a long history of use in L2 learning (see *Modern Language Journal* review by Salaberry, 2001). Language laboratories featuring audio and video material first became standard features of a modern language program during the 1970s. In the past two decades, increasing efforts have been devoted to the development of computer software for the specific purpose of supplementing classroom instruction of an L2. Studies have shown that computer-assisted language learning (CALL) offers a number of benefits. In terms of administration, technology can conserve resources, reducing time spent on student testing and evaluation. Particularly significant is the potential improvement in teacher efficiency through eliminating large quantities of repetitive grading tasks, thus freeing teachers to spend more time in personal interaction and class planning.

At Notre Dame, 80% of students live in residence halls networked with dedicated Ethernet connections, providing students with high-speed access to the campus network and the Internet. Owing to the high degree of networking across campus, this was as an ideal location to implement an electronic workbook, because technical difficulties, particularly involving slow transmission speeds, would be minimal. The Spanish language program at Notre Dame is one of the largest programs at the university, enrolling over 700 students each semester in the basic language classes alone. Language class levels 101 and 102[1] were targeted for implementation of an electronic workbook. Taught primarily by graduate teaching assistants, levels 101 and 102 consist of beginners and "false beginners" who are assigned to this level by the placement exam. Each semester, nearly 250 students enroll in these two levels, which cover the first and second halves of the textbook *¿Sabías que...?* (VanPatten et al., 2003).

In the past few years, a new breed of Web-based learning and course administration programs has emerged as the cutting edge in educational technology. These integrated learning programs allow instructors to enhance existing courses with Web-based material and offer students much more flexibility in access to course material, activities, and background information. A number of integrated learning packages were reviewed before choosing WebCT, because it appeared to offer a good selection of tools suited to the Windows environment.

Structured Input Online

The intention of implementing the electronic SI workbook in the Spanish program was to increase student exposure to target language input. This was accomplished through replacing SI activities formerly assigned as classwork and homework with integrated audio, images, and text-based SI activities online. The students could access these activities at any time, eliminating the need to visit language laboratories or sign out audio-visual material. Web-based activities allow students to receive immediate feedback on each activity, while simultaneously increasing instructor efficiency through reducing routine grading tasks. An additional benefit is that this allows instructors to focus class time on output activities and student-student interaction.

Approximately seven to ten SI activities were put online for each lesson in *¿Sabías que...?* (VanPatten et al., 2003), with each lesson being covered in about five to seven class periods. The same activities were assigned to each class section, with due dates listed in the syllabus. Grades were automatically recorded in an online grade book, where instructors would also manually insert grades for written homework, compositions, and tests. Instructors quickly familiarized themselves with the SI workbook and were able to incorporate it easily as

---

[1]During the first year of implementation, *¿Sabias que...?* and the electronic workbook were also used in level 103; hence, survey results from the first year also include respondents from 103.

a supplement to classroom activities. The online grading and automatic compilation of grades for each student were advantageous to the instructors. Less time spent grading homework assignments containing word-level and short-answer responses meant more time for lesson planning and evaluating lengthier assignments such as written compositions.

During one of the first class hours of each semester, instructors gave an orientation to the online workbook. In most cases, orientation was held in a computer-equipped classroom or laboratory. In addition, each student received a brief handout as part of the syllabus package. The handout described how to access SI activities online and included tips on troubleshooting common technical problems including software incompatibility. With only a few icons on the home page, the SI workbook was relatively straightforward. Student familiarity with computers and the simple point-and-click format prevented any reports of confusion in regard to navigation.

Student Survey Results

To evaluate the online SI workbook, student surveys were conducted at the end of the first semester of use (November 2000) and the end of the fourth semester (May 2002). A total of 223 students from levels 101, 102, and 103[2] responded to the first survey, giving a response rate of 46%. The second survey polled students from levels 101 and 102 only. The response rate was higher at 63%, with a total of 133 students responding.

Access to Online SI activities

The students using the SI workbook described themselves as expert or intermediate users of technology. Only 1% stated that they had no experience. Furthermore, when asked their opinion of online distribution of these activities, 73% were in favor of such a move. Student access to computers and Web page loading time did not appear to be a deterrent to student use. Ninety-five percent of students reported that they were able to get access to a computer either any time or almost any time they needed it. The remaining 5% of students stated that they had access to a computer part of the time. During the first semester, 32% said that the loading speed was very fast, and 58% stated that the pages appeared at an OK speed. By the fourth semester, after the server upgrade, 43% stated that the pages appeared very quickly and 50% at an OK speed. Overall, 90% of students in the first survey reported that the online SI activities were "pretty easy" to "extremely easy" to use. This percentage improved to 95% after the second survey.

From the beginning, students were able to access the SI activity Web site easily. During the first semester, 90% of students were able to log on to the Web site within three attempts. After the second survey, 96% percent of students were able to log on successfully the first time. After logging on, over 80% of students initially reported no further problems with logging in and either minimal or no technical difficulty with the SI activities at all. By the fourth semester, ease of use improved further, with almost 90% of students having no problems logging on

[2]*¿Sabías que...?* was also used in 103 during the Fall semester of 2000.

and minimal or no technical difficulty. These statistics reveal no significant impediment to online SI activity use but rather an overwhelming ease of use, even during the first semester of implementation. The statistics regarding ease of use are important, since student reactions to SI activities could be prejudiced by technical problems or unfamiliarity with the media involved. However, the overwhelming positive student response, coupled with lack of any serious technical difficulties, lays to rest this concern.

Educational Content

The survey also evaluated student experience with the online SI activity electronic workbook in terms of content. Online SI activities were used to replace some classroom SI activities and SI-focused homework assignments that would previously have been graded by the teacher. As such, it was important to evaluate the overall contribution of the activities, presented in this new format, to student learning.

In both surveys, approximately 75% of students indicated that the electronic SI activities complemented the textbook well or extremely well. In the second survey, an additional 5% of students added comments specifically stating that the online SI activities were a useful supplement to classroom and/or textbook activities. Although there are no statistics on traditional paper SI activities, these percentages lend support to the idea that little (if any) benefit was lost by the replacement of traditional paper-pen SI activities with SI online. It should be noted that there is no reason to think that a survey of student opinion regarding traditionally mediated SI activities of identical content would yield significantly different results.

These results mirror online workbook survey results found in other disciplines (see, for example, Morss, 1999; Maki et al., 2000; Henly and Reid, 2001). Despite the fact that learners saw only seven to ten of these SI activities per textbook chapter, an average of 79% of students (on both surveys) indicated that the online SI activities affected their learning to some degree. Students wrote a number of positive comments regarding the content. In addition to many general statements about the usefulness and helpfulness of the activities, specific benefits highlighted by the students included the following.

- Activities were a good compliment to classwork and textbook. (noted by 5% of students)
- Website audio to accompany activities was particularly helpful. (3%)
- Quick feedback enables students to learn from their mistakes and repeat the activities correctly. (3%)

Results

Results from the student surveys for online SI workbook use in the Spanish program at Notre Dame are summarized in Figures 6.2 and 6.3. As indicated, the first survey was conducted in December 2000, after one semester of implementation, and the second survey was conducted in May 2002, after four semesters of use. The average student responses to the six questions related to technology are displayed in Figure 6.2. Although the multiple-choice responses varied from question to question, in each case the first response was equivalent

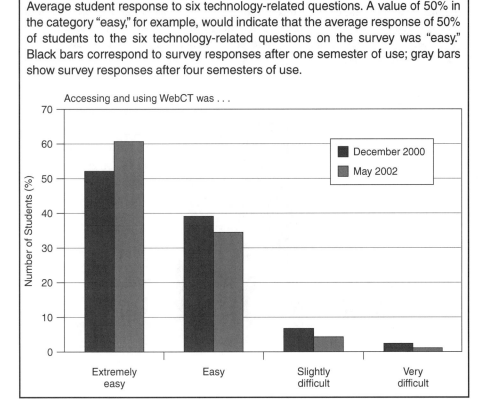

Average student response to six technology-related questions. A value of 50% in the category "easy," for example, would indicate that the average response of 50% of students to the six technology-related questions on the survey was "easy." Black bars correspond to survey responses after one semester of use; gray bars show survey responses after four semesters of use.

FIGURE 6.2

to "extremely easy," the second to "easy," the third to "slightly difficult," and the fourth response to "very difficult." This was true in all cases except if there were only three possible responses, in which case the third response was categorized as "extremely difficult." This plot shows combined results for all six questions on technology.

Figure 6.2 reveals two key conclusions regarding this particular implementation of online technology for SI-focused language instruction. First, a common concern during the initial stages of implementing language-learning activities in a new format is that students' unfamiliarity with the software and/or technology may initially limit their performance and learning. However, Figure 6.2 clearly indicates that very few students (less than 10%) encountered significant difficulty in access and use of the SI workbook even during the first semester of implementation. Second, through rapid response to reported problems, results also show that technical difficulties were greatly improved by the fourth semester. By that time only a minimal number of students (less than 5%) reported encountering significant difficulties with use of the technology. These results help settle potential concerns over the possibility of adverse effects from using technology to administer SI.

Average student response to three questions related to the educational content of the electronic workbook. Black bars indicate responses from first survey after one semester of use, while gray bars show responses for second survey after four semesters of use.

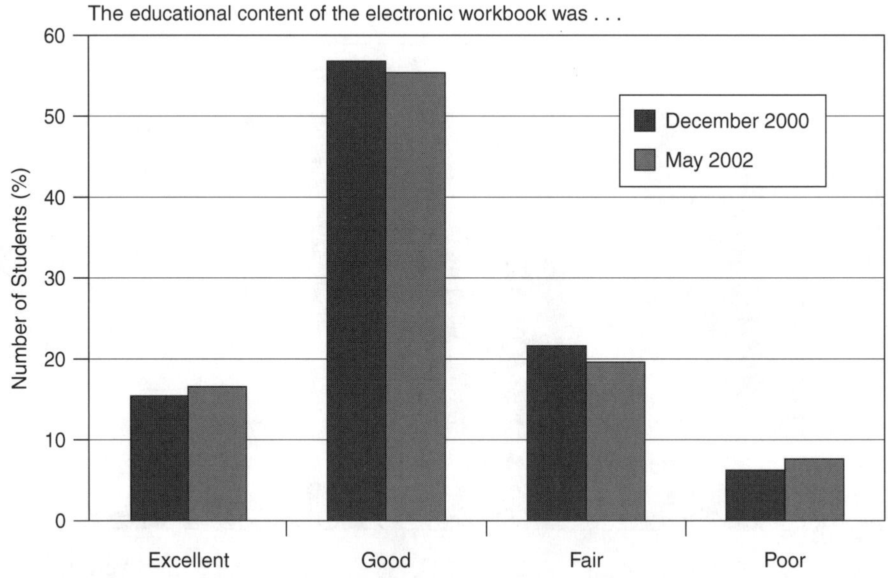

The educational content of the electronic workbook was . . .

FIGURE 6.3

In Figure 6.3, average student responses for the three questions related to the educational content of the electronic SI workbook are summarized. Although the multiple-choice responses varied from question to question, in each case the first response was equivalent to "excellent," the second to "good," the third to "fair," and the fourth response to "poor." This plot shows combined results for all three questions on SI workbook content. As shown in Figure 6.3, a majority of student responses (with a combined total of more than 70%) related to the content of the online workbook were "good" or "excellent." This is positive news, because it indicates that the SI activities are making a contribution that students are consciously aware of. Highlighted areas included the activities' compatibility with classroom and textbook material, the ability for students to receive immediate feedback on errors while working with grammatical features, and the ability to listen to audio outside of class. However, Figure 6.3 also shows significant areas for improvement. Ideally, one would prefer the majority of students to respond that the quality and the content of the activities were "excellent," rather than "good." Even more important, however, are the 20% of students who rated the electronic workbook as "fair," and the 6–7% who rated it as "poor."

In view of these latter results, it must be noted that the Web-based SI activities were intended solely to replace routine homework assignments. Educational expectations for the electronic SI workbook were that it would give a preliminary introduction to major grammatical features and provide additional reading and listening practice. The online SI activities were never expected to be the *sole* tool to bring about learning. Activities in this limited quantity cannot bring about the same benefits gained from the hours of interaction with other students and an instructor that occur every week. For this reason I would hypothesize that, when compared with a similar amount of traditionally mediated SI homework activities, the electronic workbook would be deemed equally effective or perhaps even slightly more effective. In short, the quantity (not the quality or nature) of the activities may account for some student responses regarding content. In future surveys, the educational impact of the full range of tools used in language teaching should be evaluated individually. This will isolate student response to various teaching tools and enable accurate comparisons between class activities (both SI as well as other types), written homework (traditionally mediated SI and other types), and Web-based assignments of all types.

Conclusions

As this study has shown, it is quite plausible for SI activities to be offered online, independent of classroom time (see also Sanz and Morgan-Short, 2003). With the current emphasis on computer-assisted language learning, interactive multimedia materials such as Web-based workbooks are becoming more readily available. These materials, typically textbook supplements, can be completed outside of normal classroom time. The SI approach to L2 grammar instruction can be easily delivered electronically, providing both written SI activities and opportunities to interpret oral SI recorded and played as audio files. Conversely, output-focused activities are best implemented when a context is provided for learners to exchange new information and express meaning orally with one another. These two instructional interventions (SI and output-focused practice) can be seen as complementary with each carrying its own distinct advantage. Whereas SI activities might easily function as a precursor to classroom contact hours, output-focused instruction provides the benefits of interaction between learners during regular class time.

Implementation of an electronic workbook of SI activities in the Spanish language program at Notre Dame resulted in a number of benefits. Students felt that the SI activities were a good complement to the book and the material presented in class. They also appreciated the additional flexibility afforded by electronic media that linked text and audio components, varying the type of input they could receive outside the classroom. Placing homework activities on the Web was convenient for the students, providing them with easy access to SI activities and opportunities to listen to a native speaker. Finally, automation of the grading process improved instructor efficiency, reducing time spent on routine tasks such as the grading of SI-focused homework that was previously carried out by hand.

FINAL REMARKS ON BOTH STUDIES

Through examining these two studies, we have seen how research can enhance our understanding of the way learners acquire language features and their own perception of which instructional approaches are useful to their learning experience. A number of studies dating back over thirty years have clearly documented the fact that learners move through a concrete set of developmental stages in acquiring an L2. In the past, instructional efforts have failed to "leap-frog" learners over any of these stages. However, as we saw in the first study, SI was able to bring about learner production of a form for which they were theoretically "unready."

The second study afforded us the opportunity to ask the students themselves how they believed SI activities outside the classroom contributed to their learning experience and whether converting the traditional written workbook into electronic format was conducive to learning. Results of this study showed that students did feel that SI activities complemented the instruction they were receiving in the classroom, and the increased flexibility and access to audio material provided by the electronic format was an added benefit.

READ MORE ABOUT IT

Farley, A. P., & McCollam Wiebe, K. (2005). Learner readiness and L2 Spanish: Processability theory on trial. *Estudios de lingüística aplicadoa.* Número 40.

Johnston, M. (1995). *Stages of acquisition of Spanish as a second language.* University of Western Sydney, Macarthur: The National Languages and Literacy Institute of Australia, Language Acquisition Research Centre.

Pienemann, M. (1998). *Language processing and second language development.* Amsterdam/Philadelphia: John Benjamins Publishing Company.

acquisition: the process (largely unconscious) by which a mental representation of a language system is developed in the learner.

attentional resources: the "space" available to learners in their working memory that enables storage of data during on-line comprehension.

developing system: the term used to describe the place where a learner's form-meaning connections are stored; the internalized representation of language that is developed either consciously or unconsciously (or both) in a language learner; the terms *developing system, mental representation of language,* and *linguistic system* are interchangeable.

inner speech: a "self talk" or interior rehearsing of what later becomes audible output. This term is used within a Vygotskian sociocultural approach to language acquisition.

input: the raw linguistic data (oral or written) to which learners are exposed. Learners attend to input with a primary focus on getting meaning from it.

input processing: refers to the set of real-time processes by which input is filtered and may be converted into intake. Input processing is only one set of processes involved in first or second language acquisition. Partial or total form-meaning connections can occur during this process.

intake: this term was first coined by Corder; in this book, intake is defined as the subset of filtered input that is made available for further processing. Intake is held in working memory during the act of comprehension. In other words, intake is processed input that may or may not enter the developing system.

meaning-based output instruction: a type of instruction that provides both explicit information and structured output activities that give learners opportunities to create meaning. As with structured input activities, structured output activities are designed to make the target item more salient to the learner. Although similar to more traditional instruction in its focus on production, meaning-based output instruction is not merely mechanical in nature.

mnemonics: from the Greek word *mnemon* (mindful). Mnemonics are ways or "devices" (mental pictures, stories, and so on) used for remembering a list of unrelated items in a particular order.

noticing: the simple act of recognizing that a feature exists. Often a form in the input may be noticed but still not subsequently processed.

output: oral or written language that a learner produces to express meaning.

primacy effects: when a form is more salient and therefore held in working memory more easily because it is heard or read first (or near the beginning) in a series of forms.

processing instruction: a type of focus-on-form grammar instruction in which learners are given (1) explicit information about a linguistic structure or form, (2) explicit information about less-than optimal learner processing strategies that may hinder or prevent the processing of a target form, and (3) structured input activities designed to deter learners from using inferior processing strategies and instead use more beneficial ones.

readiness: a construct within the Pienemann (1998) framework that refers to an L2 learner's state relative to features higher in the hierarchy of processability. Readiness for a particular structure means that a learner already possesses the processing procedures needed to produce L2 features that correspond to all previous stages.

recency effects: when a form is more salient and therefore held in working memory more easily because it is heard or read last (or near the end) in a series of forms.

redundancy: when two or more elements in an utterance or discourse encode the same semantic information (meaning).

structured input: a term first coined by Lee and VanPatten (1995). Structured input activities push learners away from less-than-optimal strategies that they take to the task of L2 processing and toward more beneficial processing strategies. To qualify as structured input, activity items (and an activity as a whole) must adhere to all the guidelines for SI activity design articulated in Lee and VanPatten (1995), VanPatten (1996), and this book. Most importantly, authentic structured input activities take into account VanPatten's (1996, 2003) principles and subprinciples, expounded on here in Chapters 2, 3, and 4.

structured output: this term was first coined by Lee and VanPatten (1995). Structured output activities give learners an opportunity to express ideas, opinions, beliefs, and so on, in a meaningful context. To qualify as structured output, activity items (and an activity as a whole) must adhere to all the guidelines for structured output activity design articulated in Lee and VanPatten (1995).

traditional instruction: in this book, this term refers to the typical approach to second language teaching that involves the progression from mechanical drills to meaningful drills to communicative drills.

task demands: what a particular language activity requires of the learner.

REFERENCES

Alanen, R. (1995). Input enhancement and rule presentation in second language acquisition. In R. Schmidt (ed.), *Attention and awareness in foreign language learning*. Manoa, HI: Second Language Teaching & Curriculum Center. 305–358.

Barcroft, J., & VanPatten, B. (1997). Acoustic salience of grammatical forms: The effect of location, stress, and boundedness on Spanish L2 input processing. In A. Perez-Leroux & W. R. Glass (eds.), *Contemporary perspectives on the acquisition of Spanish: Production, processing, and comprehension*. Somerville, MA: Cascadilla Press. 109–121.

Bardovi-Harlig, K. (1992). The use of adverbials and natural order in the development of temporal expression. *International Review of Applied Linguistics* 30: 299–320.

Bates, E., & MacWhinney, B. (1982). Functionalist approaches to grammar. In E. Wanner & L. Gleitman (eds.), *Language acquisition: The state of the art*. New York: Cambridge University Press.

Bates, E., & MacWhinney, B. (1989). Functionalism and the competition model. In B. MacWhinney & E. Bates (eds.), *The cross-linguistic study of sentence processing*. Cambridge: Cambridge University Press. 77–117.

Bavin, E. L., & Shopen, T. (1989). Cues to sentence interpretation in Warlpiri. In B. MacWhinney & E. Bates (eds.), *The cross-linguistic study of sentence processing*. Cambridge: Cambridge University Press. 185–205.

Benati, A. (2001). A comparative study of the effects of processing instruction and output-based instruction on the acquisition of the Italian future tense. *Language Teaching Research* 5: 95–127.

Benati, A. (2004). The effects of structured input activities and explicit information on the acquisition of the Italian future tense. In B. VanPatten (ed.), *Processing instruction: Theory, research, and commentary*. Mahwah, NJ: Erlbaum. 207–226.

Berne, J. (1992). *The effects of text type, assessment task, and target language experience on foreign language learners' performance on listening comprehension tests*. Unpublished doctoral dissertation, The University of Illinois at Urbana-Champaign.

Binkowski, D. D. (1992). *The effects of attentional focus, presentation mode, and language experience on second language learner's sentence processing*. Unpublished doctoral thesis, University of Illinois at Urbana-Champaign.

Blau, E. K. (1990). The effect of syntax, speed and pauses on listening comprehension. *TESOL Quarterly* 24: 746–753.

Bransdorfer, R. (1989). *Processing function words in input: Does meaning make a difference?* Paper presented at the annual meeting of the American Association of Teachers of Spanish and Portuguese, San Antonio, TX.

Bransdorfer, R. (1991). *Communicative value and linguistic knowledge in second language oral input processing.* Unpublished doctoral thesis, University of Illinois at Urbana-Champaign.

Buck, M. (2000). *Procesamiento del lenguaje y adquisición de una segunda lengua. Un estudio de la adquisición de un punto gramatical en inglés por hispanohablantes.* Unpublished doctoral thesis, Universidad Nacional Autónoma de México.

Cadierno, T. (1995). Formal instruction from a processing perspective: An investigation into the Spanish past tense. *Modern Language Journal* 79: 179–193.

Cheng, A. (1995). *Grammar instruction and input processing: The acquisition of Spanish* ser *and* estar. Unpublished doctoral dissertation, University of Illinois at Urbana-Champaign, Urbana, IL.

Chomsky, N. (1965). *Aspects of the theory of syntax.* Cambridge, MA: MIT Press.

Chomsky, N. (1981). *Lectures on government and binding.* Dordrecht: Foris.

Collentine, J. G. (1993). *The development of complex syntax and the selection of mood by foreign language learners of Spanish.* Unpublished doctoral dissertation, University of Texas at Austin, Austin, TX.

Collentine, J. G. (1995). The development of complex syntax and mood-selection abilities by intermediate-level learners of Spanish. *Hispania* 78: 122–136.

Collentine, J. G. (1997). Irregular verbs and noticing the Spanish subjunctive. *Spanish Applied Linguistics,* 1: 3–23.

Collentine, J. G. (1998). Processing instruction and the subjunctive. *Hispania* 81: 576–587.

Collentine, J. G. (2002). On the acquisition of the subjunctive and authentic processing instruction: A response to Farley. *Hispania* 85: 900–909.

DeKeyser, R. M., Salaberry, R, Robinson, P., & Harrington, M. (2002). What gets processed in processing instruction: A response to Bill VanPatten's "Update." *Language Learning* 52: 805–823.

Doughty, C. (1991). Second language instruction does make a difference: Evidence from an empirical study of SL relativization. *Studies in Second Language Acquisition* 13: 431–469.

Ellis, R. (1990). *Instructed second language acquisition.* Oxford: Basil Blackwell.

Ellis, R. (1997). *SLA research and language teaching.* Oxford: Oxford University Press.

Ervin-Tripp, S. M. (1974). Is second language learning really like the first? *TESOL Quarterly* 8: 111–127.

Faerch, C., & Kasper, G. (1986). The role of comprehension in second language learning. *Applied Linguistics* 7: 257–274.

Farley, A. P. (2001a). Authentic processing instruction and the Spanish subjunctive. *Hispania* 84: 289–299.

Farley, A. P. (2001b). Processing instruction and meaning-based output instruction: A comparative study. *Spanish Applied Linguistics.* December, 2001.

Farley, A. P. (2002). Processing instruction, communicative value, and ecological validity: A response to Collentine's defense. *Hispania* 85: 889–895.

Farley, A. P. (2004a). Processing instruction and meaning-based output instruction. In B. VanPatten (ed.), *Processing instruction: Theory, research, and commentary.* Mahwah, NJ: Erlbaum. 143–168.

Farley, A. P. (2004b). Processing instruction and the Spanish subjunctive: Is explicit information needed? In B. VanPatten (ed.), *Processing instruction: Theory, research, and commentary.* Mahwah, NJ: Erlbaum. 227–240.

Farley, A. P., & McCollam Wiebe, K. (2005). Learner readiness and L2 Spanish: Processability theory on trial. *Estudios de lingüística aplicada.* Número 40. (in press)

Feustle, J. A. (2000). *¿Sabías que ...? Cuaderno de trabajo electrónico.* New York: McGraw-Hill.

Feustle, J. (2001). Extending the reach of the classroom with Web-based programs. *Hispania* 84: 837–849.

Gass, S. M. (1989). How do learners resolve linguistic conflicts? In S. Gass & J. Schacter (eds.), *Linguistic perspectives on second language acquisition.* Cambridge: Cambridge University Press. 183–199.

Gass, S. M. (1997) *Input, interaction, and the second language learner.* Mahwah, NJ: Erlbaum.

Glass, W. R. (1994). Paper delivered at the annual meeting of the American Association for Applied Linguistics, Baltimore, MD.

Glisan, E. (1985). The effect of word order on listening comprehension and pattern retention: An experiment in Spanish as a foreign language. *Language Learning* 35: 443–472.

Henly, D., & Reid, A. (2001). Use of the Web to provide learning support for a large metabolism and nutrition class. *Biochemistry and Molecular Biology Education* 29: 229–233.

Hulstijn, J., & DeGraaf, R. (1994). Under what conditions does explicit knowledge of a second language facilitate the acquisition of implicit knowledge? A research proposal. *AILA Review* 11: 97–112.

Issidorides, D. C., & Hulstijn, J. H. (1992). Comprehension of grammatically modified and nonmodified sentences by second language learners. *Applied Psycholinguistics* 13: 147–171.

Johnston, M. (1995). *Stages of acquisition of Spanish as a second language.* University of Western Sydney, Macarthur: The National Languages and Literacy Institute of Australia, Language Acquisition Research Centre.

Just, M. A., & Carpenter, P. A. (1993). A capacity theory of comprehension: Individual differences in working memory. *Psychological Review* 99: 122–149.

Kim, Jong-Bok. 1995. *The grammar of negation: A lexicalist, constraint-based perspective.* Unpublished doctoral dissertation, Stanford University.

Klein, W. (1986). *Second language acquisition.* Cambridge: Cambridge University Press.

Krashen, S. (1980). The input hypothesis. In J. Alatis (ed.), *Current issues in bilingual education.* Washington, D.C.: Georgetown University Press. 168–180.

Krashen, S. (1982). *Second language acquisition and second language learning.* London: Longman.

Krashen, S. D. (1982). *Principles and practice in second language acquisition.* Oxford: Pergamon Press.

Larsen-Freeman, D., & Long, M. H. (1991). *Introduction to second language acquisition research.* London: Longman.

Lee, J. F. (1987a) The Spanish subjunctive: An information processing perspective. *The Modern Language Journal* 71: 50–57.

Lee, J. F. (1987b). Morphological factors influencing pronominal reference assignment by learners of Spanish. In T. A. Morgan, J. F. Lee, & B. VanPatten (eds.), *Language and language use: Studies in Spanish.* Lanham, MD: University Press of America. 221–232.

Lee, J. F., Cadierno, T., Glass, W. R., & VanPatten, B. (1997). *Processing tense in second language input: Lexical cues versus grammatical cues.* The University of Illinois at Urbana-Champaign.

Lee, J., & VanPatten, B. (1995). *Making communicative language teaching happen.* New York: McGraw-Hill.

Lee, J., & VanPatten, B. (2003). *Making communicative language teaching happen* (2d ed). New York: McGraw-Hill.

Lightbown, P., & Spada, N. (1999). Instruction, first language influence, and developmental readiness in second language acquisition. *The Modern Language Journal* 83: 1–22.

LoCoco, V. (1987). Learner comprehension of oral and written sentences in German and Spanish: The importance of word order. In B. VanPatten, T. R. Dvorak, & James F. Lee (eds.), *Foreign language learning: A research perspective* Cambridge, MA: Newbury House. 119–129.

Long, M. (1981). Input, interaction, and second language interaction. In H. Winitz (ed.), *Native language and foreign language acquisition.* Annals of the New York Academy of Sciences 379: 259–278.

Long, M. (1983). Native-speaker/non-native speaker conversation and the negotiation of comprehensible input. *Applied Linguistics* 4: 126–141.

Maki, R. H., Maki, W. S., Patterson, M., & Whittaker, P. D. (2000). Evaluation of a Web-based introductory psychology course: I. Learning and satisfaction in on-line versus lecture courses. *Behavior Research Methods: Instruments & Computers* 32: 230–239.

Mangubhai, F. (1991) The processing behaviors of adult second language learners and their relationship to second language proficiency. *Applied Linguistics* 12: 268–297.

McDonald, J. L., & Heilenman, L. K. (1992). Changes in sentence processing as second language proficiency increases. In R. J. Harris (ed.), *Cognitive processing in bilinguals.* Elsevier. 325–336.

Morss, D. (1999). A study of student perspectives on Web-based learning: WebCT in the classroom. *Internet Research: Electronic Networking Applications and Policy* 9: 393–408.

Musumeci, D. (1989). *The ability of second language learners to assign tense at the sentence level.* Unpublished doctoral dissertation, University of Illinois at Urbana-Champaign.

Nam, E. (1975). Child and adult perceptual strategies in second language acquisition. Paper presented at the 1975 TESOL Convention, Los Angeles, CA.

Neisser, U. (1967). *Cognitive psychology.* New York, NY: Appleton.

Pereira, I. (1996). *Markedness and instructed SLA: An experiment in teaching the Spanish subjunctive.* Unpublished doctoral dissertation, University of Illinois at Urbana-Champaign, Urbana, IL.

Peters, A. M. (1985). Language segmentation: Operating principles for the perception and analysis of language. In D. Slobin (ed.), *The cross-linguistic study of language acquisition,* vol. 2. Hillsdale, NJ: Erlbaum. 1029–1067.

Pica, T. (1994). Research on negotiation: What does it reveal about second language learning conditions, processes, and outcomes? *Language Learning* 44: 493–527.

Pienemann, M. (1998). *Language processing and second language development.* Amsterdam/Philadelphia: John Benjamins Publishing Company.

Pléh, C. (1989). The development of sentence interpretation in Hungarian. In B. MacWhinney & E. Bates (eds.), *The cross-linguistic study of sentence processing* Cambridge: Cambridge University Press. 158–184.

Rosa, E., & O'Neill, M. (1998). Effects of stress and location on acoustic salience at the initial stages of Spanish L2 input processing. *Spanish Applied Linguistics* 2: 24–52.

Salaberry, M. R. (2001). The use of technology for second language learning and teaching: A retrospective. *Modern Language Journal* 85: 39–56.

Sanz, C., & Morgan-Short, K. (2004). Positive evidence vs. explicit rule presentation and explicit negative feedback: A computer-assisted study. *Language Learning.* 54: 35–78

Schmidt, R. (1994). Deconstructing consciousness in search of useful definitions for applied linguistics. *AILA Review* 11: 11–26.

Schmidt, R. W. (1990) The role of consciousness in second language learning. *Applied Linguistics* 11: 129–158.

Scott, V. (1989). An empirical study of explicit and implicit teaching strategies in French. *Modern Language Journal* 73: 14–22.

Sharwood Smith, M. (1986). Comprehension versus acquisition: Two ways of processing input. *Applied Linguistics* 7: 239–274.

Simard, D., & Wong, W. (2001). Alertness, orientation, and detection: The conceptualization of attentional functions in SLA. *Studies in Second Language Acquisition* 23: 71–102.

Swain, M. (1985). Communicative competence: Some roles of comprehensible input and comprehensive output in its development. In S. Gass & C. Madden (eds.), *Input in second language acquisition.* Rowley, MA: Newbury House. 235–253.

Swain, M. (1997). The output hypothesis, focus on form, and second language learning. In V. Berry, B. Adamson, & W. Littlewood. (eds.), *Applying linguistics: Insights into language in education.* 1–21.

VanPatten, B. (1984). Learner comprehension of clitic pronouns: More evidence for a word order strategy. *Hispanic Linguistics* 1: 56–66.

VanPatten, B. (1990). Attending to content and form in the input: An experiment in consciousness. *Studies in Second Language Acquisition* 12: 287–301.

VanPatten, B. (1996). *Input processing and grammar instruction: Theory and research.* Norwood, NJ: Ablex.

VanPatten, B. (2003). *From input to output: A teacher's guide to second language acquisition.* New York: McGraw-Hill.

VanPatten, B., ed. (2004). *Processing instruction: Theory, research, and commentary.* Mahwah, NJ: Erlbaum.

VanPatten, B., & Cadierno, T. (1993). Input processing and second language acquisition: A role for instruction. *Modern Language Journal* 77: 45–57.

VanPatten, B., & Fernández, C. (2004). The long-term effects of processing instruction. In VanPatten, B. (ed.), *Processing instruction: Theory, research, and commentary.* Mahwah, NJ: Erlbaum.

VanPatten, B., & Houston, T. (1998). Contextual effects in processing L2 input sentences. *Spanish Applied Linguistics* 2: 53–70.

VanPatten, B., Lee, J., & Ballman, T. (2000). *¿Sabías que ...?* 3d ed. New York: McGraw-Hill.

VanPatten, B., & Oikennon, S. (1996). Explanation versus structured input in processing instruction. *Studies in Second Language Acquisition* 18: 495–510.

VanPatten, B., & Sanz, C. (1995). From input to output: Processing instruction and communicative tasks. In F. Eckman, D. Highland, P. W. Lee, J. Mileham, & R. R. Weber (eds.). *Second language acquisition theory and pedagogy.* Hillsdale, NJ: Erlbaum. 169–185.

VanPatten, B., & Wong, W. (2003). Processing instruction and the French causative: A replication. In B. VanPatten (ed.), *Processing instruction: Theory, research, and commentary.* Mahwah, NJ: Erlbaum.

Vygotsky, L. (1962). *Thought and language.* Cambridge, MA: MIT Press.

Wong, W. (2002). Linking form and meaning: Processing instruction. *The French Review* 76: 2.

Wong, W. (2004). Processing instruction in French: The roles of explicit information and structured input. In B. VanPatten (ed.), *Processing instruction: Theory, research, and commentary.* Mahwah, NJ: Erlbaum. 187–206.

Page numbers followed by "t" refer to tables

accuracy, promotion of with SI activities, 90

accusative noun phrase, in Spanish, 62

acquisition, defined, 109

adverbial expressions, may communicate subtleties that are also marked morphologically, 19

adverbials of time
separated from targeted verb form, 29, 30, 31, 33, 35
used rather than verb endings to determine tense, 22

affective activities, 26
allow for numerous possible answers, 46, 49
allow learners to observe target forms in meaningful contexts, 87
follow-up steps, 53
for German past tense, 34–35
for Italian future tense, 29–31
for object marker *a*, 96
for object pronouns in Spanish, 64–67
for Spanish subjunctive, 49–51
for subject-verb agreement in English, 36–37
for subjunctive, 97

attentional resources, 24
defined, 4, 109

Audiolingualism, 1

aural input, 64
contextualized interpretation practice, 33
importance of, 48
often neglected by foreign language instructors, 78
structured input (SI) activities in, 87

Availability of Resources Principle, 6, 8–9, 21, 24–25

"bad" input, 83, 84

Barcroft, J., 44

Bardovi-Harlig, K., 23

Bates, E., 2–3

Bavin, E. L., 61

behavioristic approaches, 1–2

Benati, A., 39, 40–41

Berne, J., 24–25

binary option, 15

Blackboard, 91

Bransdorfer, R., 23–24

Cadierno, T., 22, 39, 71

case markers, 10

Chomsky, Noam: Universal Grammar, 3, 5

collaboration, with other instructors on SI activities, 87–89

Collentine, Joseph, 45, 82–83

Competition Model, 3

comprehensible input, 2, 24

computer-assisted language learning, 90–91, 101–2, 107

connected discourse, 14, 78–79

content words
more acoustically salient than other elements, 7
roots typically stressed more than grammatical affixes, 21
tendency for learners to process before anything else, 7, 20–22

Contextual Constraint Principle, 9, 10, 59, 60

contextual information, role in processing of clauses containing OVS word order, 10

corrective feedback, 89–90

course management programs, 90–91, 102
creativity, maintaining through collaboration, 87–89

developing system, 6
    defined, 109
developmental stages, of L2 learning, 92–93, 108
direct object pronoun, misinterpreted in sentence-initial position, 43

electronic workbook formats, 91, 102
    access and use of, 105
    educational content, 104, 106t
    as or more effective than traditional SI homework activities, 107
English
    marked by lexical items, 19
    subject-verb agreement in, 36–37
    subject-verb-object (SVO) word order, 58–59
    third person singular form, 36, 38
English-as-Second Language (ESL) learners
    developmental stages, 93
    greater comprehension of input with pauses than with slower or simpler input, 25
Ervin-Tripp, S. M., 60
Event Probabilities Principle, 9, 10, 59, 60
explicit instruction (EI), 40–41, 60–61, 89–90.
    See also processing instruction (SI + EI)
explicit subject
    removed from activity items, 36–37
    separated from target verb form, 30

Farley, A.
    "Authentic processing instruction and the Spanish subjunctive," 55–56
    learner reactions to SI activities on-line, 101–7
    Learner readiness and L2 Spanish: Processability theory on trial, 92–108
    "Processing instruction and meaning-based instruction: A comparative study," 56–57
feedback
    corrective, 89–90
    in follow-up steps, 62
    for on-line SI activities, xii
    as result of output, 4, 5
filler words, 7
final sentence position, processed second, 9
first language (L1) acquisition, research on, 20–25, 44
First Noun Principle, 9–11, 43
    conditions when overridden, 10, 59, 61
    Contextual Constraint Principle, 9, 10, 59, 60
    Event Probabilities Principle, 9, 10, 59, 60
    evidenced in L2 learners with a number of different native languages, 60
    in first language acquisition, 61
    grammatical forms affected by, 60, 61t
    Lexical Semantics Principle, 9, 10, 59, 60
    object pronouns in German, 67–70
    object pronouns in Spanish, 60, 62–67
    and passive constructions, 60
    principles in practice, 71
    referential activities to help learners avoid reliance on, 62–64
    research, 60–62
    sample studies, 71–72
    summary of research supporting, 11
focus-on-form, xi
follow-up steps
    feedback, 62
    repeating activity in light of a new context, 53
    in structured input (SI) activities, 32, 38, 53
Foreign Language Teaching Methodology courses, xi
formal structure, 3
form-meaning connections, 3, 5, 6
free word order, 61
French
    avoir + negation, 51–54
    marked by lexical items, 19
functional structure, 3
future tense, in Italian, 26–33

Gass, S. M., 4, 61
German
    allows for both OVS and SVO word orders in main clauses, 67
    fairly strict word order, 67
    marked by lexical items, 19
    object pronouns in, 67–70
    past tense in, 33–35
"giveaway" vocabulary, 84–85
Glass, W. R., 22
grammar
    as significant factor in student learning, 91
    Universal, 3, 5
grammar-driven exercises, 75–76
grammar instruction, approaches to, 89
grammatical forms
    affected by First Noun Principle, 60, 61t
    affected by Primacy of Meaning Principle, 19t–20

grammatical forms—*(Cont.)*
  affected by Sentence Location Principle, 43t–44
  tendency to rely on lexical cues as opposed to, 18
grammaticality judgment task (GJT), 98

habit-formation, 1
Heilenman, L. K., 61
Hispania, 56
Houston, T., 61–62
Hulstijn, J., 61

images, in SI activities, 63–64, 68–69
information gap activities, 15
initial sentence position
  elements processed first, 9
  elements processed more easily than other elements, 44, 65
  misinterpretation of direct object pronoun in, 43
  targeted forms in, 28, 30, 31, 35, 36
innate linguistic system, 3
inner speech, 5
  defined, 4, 109
input
  "bad," 83, 84
  and Competition Model, 3
  comprehensible, 2, 24
  defined, 1, 109
  essentially drives second language acquisition, 83
  having learners do something with, 35, 77–78
  history of perspectives on, 1–3
  importance of, 1
  interaction with innate principles, 3
  structuring, 26, 52
  use of both oral and written, 15
input flooding, 89
Input Hypothesis, 2
input processing
  defined, 5–6, 109
  and learner's processing strategies, 15
Input Processing Model, 3, 5–11
  as complimentary to output production processes, 86
  structured input based on, 12
intake, 89
  defined, 6, 109
interaction
  with innate principles, 3
  negotiated, 4, 5

oral, 33
  requests for clarification during, 4
interactive course management programs, 90–91
interactive multimedia materials, 107
interlanguage, 4, 5
internal grammar, 5
interpretation
  effect of PI on, 40–41, 86
  effect of SI and MOI on, 56–57
  practice in aural mode, 33
  strategies, 12
Issidorides, D. C., 61
Italian
  future tense, 26–33, 39–40
  marked by lexical items, 19

Johnston, M., 94, 101

Klein, W., 44
Krashen, S. D., 2

language laboratories, 101
language production, as a means of acquisition, 4
learner readiness, 93–94
  defined, 110
  no effect on production, 101
Learner readiness and L2 Spanish: Processability theory on trial (Farley and McCollam Wiebe), 92–108
  assessing learner performance before and after instruction, 98–99
  conclusions, 101
  experimental design, 95
  frequencies of development by treatment group and structure, 100t
  instructional materials, 95–97
  results, 99–100
  summaries of all results, 100t
learning preferences, 85
Lee, J., 22, 23, 75, 86
lexical cues
  tendency to rely on as opposed to grammatical forms, 7, 18
  tendency to rely on as time indicator, 22–23, 33
  used to get meaning when grammatical forms encode the same information, 21, 22–23
Lexical Preference Principle, 6, 7, 9, 21, 22–23, 79

Lexical Semantics Principle, 9, 10, 59, 60
LoCoco, V., 60–61
low-intermediate learners, role of SI in noticing and processing of language structures, xii

MacWhinney, B., 2–3
Mangubhai, F., 21
matching activities, 15, 86
McCollam Wiebe, K., 92–108
McDonald, J. L., 61
meaning
    greatest concern of second language learners, 86
    keeping in focus, 75–76
    and syntax, 8
meaning-based output instruction (MOI), 55
    defined, 109
    and SI activities, effect on sentence-level interpretation and production tasks, 56–57
meaning-before-form processing tendency, 18, 20
Meaning-before-Nonmeaning Principle, 6, 23
meanings and forms, connections made between, 3, 5, 6
medial sentence position
    grammatical features often found in, 43
    processed last, 9
    relocation to more salient position, 47, 52
    subjunctive often located in, 45, 96
memorization, subject to both primacy and recency effects, 44
mental rehearsal, 5
mnemonics, defined, 44, 109
mood, tendency to process lexically, 19–20
morphological markers, may not be analyzed for meaning, 21
multiple-choice activities, 15, 86
Musumeci, Diane, 23, 91

Nam, E., 61
negotiated interactions, 4, 5
Neisser, U., 44
nonredundant meaningful grammatical forms, tendency to process before redundant meaningful forms, 6, 8, 21, 23
noticing, 2
    defined, 6, 109
    promoted by SI activities, xii, 35

object pronouns, 10
    effect of PI on, 71–72
    misinterpreted in sentence-initial position, 43

in Spanish, and First Noun Principle, 60, 62–67
object-verb-subject (OVS) word order, 10, 59
Oikennon, S., 72
O'Neill, M., 44
on-line comprehension, of aural and written input, xi
on-line SI activities, learner reactions to, xii, 101–7
oral input activities, 15, 48, 64, 78
oral language production, effects of PI on, 72, 86
output-focused instructional materials, 17, 86, 107
Output Hypothesis, 4
output (production) activities, 39, 55
    as a crucial component of second language acquisition, 5
    defined, 110
    lead to both self-correction and feedback from others, 4
    role of, 86
    theory and research, 4–5

paradigms, 75
partial redundancy, 19
passive constructions, 10, 60
pattern practicing, 1
Pereira, I., 45
picture description task (PDT), 98–99
    emergence and accuracy scores, 99
Pienemann, M.: Hierarchy of processing procedures, 93t, 94, 101
Pléh, C., 61
Preference for Nonredundancy Principle, 6, 8, 21, 23
primacy effect, defined, 44, 110
Primacy of Content Words Principle, 6, 20–22
    support for in studies involving L2 acquisition of German, Hindi, Spanish, and other languages, 21–25
Primacy of Meaning Principle, 6–9, 29
    Availability of Resources Principle, 6, 8–9, 21, 24–25
    future tense in Italian, 26–33
    grammatical forms affected by, 19t–20
    L1 and L2 studies conducted on, 20–25
    Lexical Preference Principle, 6, 7, 21
    Meaning-before-Nonmeaning Principle, 6, 8, 21
    and past tense in German, 33–35

Primacy of Meaning Principle—*(Cont.)*
  Preference for Nonredundancy Principle, 6, 8, 21, 23
  Primacy of Content Words Principle, 6, 7
  principles in practice, 38
  Sentence Location Principle, 7
  subject-verb agreement in English, 36–37
  supporting research, 11, 25t
  tendency to process meaning over form, 18
Principles in Practice, xii
  First Noun Principle, 71
  Primacy of Meaning Principle, 38
  Sentence Location Principle, 54–55
Processability Theory, 93
processing
  defined, 6
  difficulties based on redundancy and meaningfulness, 8t
  on a need basis, 8
processing instruction (SI + EI)
  defined, 110
  effect on processing of future forms in Italian, 39–40
  effect on tasks involving interpretation and production, 40–41
  effects on acquisition of preterite tense in Spanish, 39
  effects on oral language production, 72
  greater effect than meaning-based input on interpretation and production of Spanish subjunctive, 55–56
  greater effect than output practice alone for interpretation and oral and written production, 86
  greater effect than traditional instruction on acquisition of object pronouns, 71–72
processing problems
  of L2 learners of German with object pronouns, 68
  in noticing future forms in Italian, 26
processing strategies, of learners, keeping in mind, 79–80
production activities. *See* output (production) activities
proficiency level, 9
prosody, use in processing audible input strings, 21

Quia workbook, electronic, 91

raw (unaltered) input, 2
readiness. *See* learner readiness

recency effect, defined, 44, 110
redundancy, 2
  defined, 7, 110
  partial, 19
  and processing problems, 8t
  subjunctive markers, 20, 46
redundant meaningful forms, processed after nonredundant meaningful grammatical forms, 6, 8, 21, 23
referential activities, 26
  allow for only one correct answer, 46
  follow-up steps, 53
  force learners to attend to target form, 86–87
  for future tense in Italian, 27–28
  for German past tense, 33–34
  to help learners avoid reliance on First Noun Principle, 62–64
  ideally precede affective activities, 87
  for object marker *a,* 95–96
  require learner to focus on form, 46
  for Spanish subjunctive, 46–49
  for subject-verb agreement in English, 36–37
  for subjunctive, 96–97
repetition task, learners consistently remember first and last words, 44
Romance languages
  and Primacy of Meaning Principle, 19
  subjective markers, 20
  word order, 58
Rosa, E., 44

¿Sabías que…?, 91, 102
Sanskrit, 61
Sanz, C., 72, 91
Schmidt, R. W., 2
second language acquisition (SLA), research, xi, 1
second language (L2) learners
  acquisition of new forms, 1
  designing SI activities for, xi
  developmental stages, 92–93
  most concerned with meaning, 86
  tendency to rely on lexical cues as time indicator, 33
second language (L2) teaching, behavioristic approaches, 1–2
self-correction, 4, 5
self-talk, defined, 4
sentence-level processing, role of context, 10
Sentence Location Principle, 7, 28, 36, 79, 96
  French *avoir* + negation, 51–54
  grammatical forms affected by, 43t–44

implies that learners are sensitive to position within an utterance, 42–43, 65
research, 44–45
sample studies, 55–57
Spanish subjunctive, 45–51
Shopen, T., 61
sound-meaning connections, 33, 78
Spanish
    marked by lexical items, 19
    object pronouns, and First Noun Principle, 62–67
    processability theory applied to, 94
    SI activities presenting past tense forms, 12–13
Spanish Applied Linguistics, 57
Spanish subjunctive
    affective activities for, 49–51
    effect of PI and meaning-based input on interpretation and production of, 55–56
    often located in sentence-medial position, 45
    as a redundant feature, 46
    referential activities for, 46–49
    and Sentence Location Principle, 45–51
structure, two levels of, 3
structured input (SI)
    based on VanPatten's model of input processing, 12
    defined, 110
    summary of research on, 16t
structured input (SI) activities
    appeal to audience, 89
    attention to utterance length, 80–81
    in aural mode, 87
    can promote noticing of a form, 35
    central themes, 75–76
    charges of artificiality, 82–83
    discourse-level, 78–79
    and educational technology, 90–91
    effect on tasks involving interpretation and production, 40–41
    follow-up steps, 32, 38, 53
    form only one component of instruction, 39
    images in, 63–64
    with internet-delivered workbook format, 91
    and meaning-based output activities for sentence-level interpretation and production, 56–57
    online, 102–4
    oral, 48, 64
    promotion of accuracy, 90
    push learners to make meaning-focused decisions, 77

research on interpretation and production, 17
sensitivity to learners in topic generation, 88
should include only known vocabulary, 80
should present only one thing at a time, 28, 66
for Spanish subjunctive, 46–51
suggested themes and subtopics, 88
themes, 31
varying the format of, 85–86
structured input (SI) activity design
    collaboration with other instructors to maintain creativity, 87–89
    common pitfalls, xii, 73–85
        creating "giveaway" items through poor vocabulary choice, 84–85
        developing ungrammatical sentences as potential answers, 83–84
        feeling the need to "remain faithful" to the language, 81–83
        not attending to utterance length, 80–81
        not having learners do something with the input, 77–78
        not keeping meaning in focus, 75–76
        not keeping the learners' processing strategies in mind, 79–80
        not moving from sentence to connected discourse, 78–79
        not presenting both oral and written input, 78
        not presenting one thing at a time, 73–75
    frequently asked questions, xii, 85–91
    guidelines for, 12–17
        have learners do something with the input, 15
        keep learner's processing strategies in mind, 15
        keep meaning in focus, 13–14
        move from sentences to connected discourse, 14
        present one thing at a time, 12–13
        use both oral and written input, 15
    sensitivity to learners in topic generation, 88
    suggested themes and subtopics, 88
structured output, defined, 110
structuring the input, 26, 52
subject-verb-object (SVO) word order, 10, 58–59
subjunctives
    generally occur in sentence-medial position, 96
    markers often redundant, 20, 46
substitution drills, 1

Swain, Merrill: Output Hypothesis, 4
syntax, role in which meaning is delivered, 8

targeted form, in utterance-initial position, 28,
 30, 31, 35, 36
task demands, defined, 4, 110
technology, history of use in L2 learning, 101
textual enhancement, 89
themes, for SI activities, 88
third person singular form in English, 36, 38
time-of-event, extracted from lexical cues
 rather than verb endings, 22–23, 33
Total Physical Response (TPR) instruction, 21
traditional instruction
 compared to processing instruction in rela-
  tion to FNP, 71–72
 defined, 110
transformations drills, 1

ungrammatical sentences, as potential
 answers in instructional activities, 83–84
Universal Grammar (UG), 3, 5
University of Notre Dame
 Spanish language program, 102
 web-based platform for delivery of SI activities, 91
utterance length, 9
 attending to, 80–81
 and exhaustion of working memory, 14

VanPatten, B.
 argument that likelihood of form being
  processed increases with increased comprehensibility, 24
 "Attending to content and form in the
  input: An experiment in consciousness,"
  21–22
 "Contextual effects in processing L2 input
  sentences," 61–62

"Explanation versus structured input in
 processing instruction," 72, 74–75
five subprinciples pertaining to meaning-
 before-form processing tendency, 20
"From input to output: Processing instruction and communicative tasks," 72, 86
guidelines for successful design of SI activities, 12–17, 15, 16t, 28, 38, 66, 73
*Input processing and grammar instruction:
 Theory and research*, 25
"Input processing and second language
 acquisition: A role for instruction," 71
Input Processing Model, 3, 5–11
on limitations of learners' working
 memory, 42
*Making communicative language teaching hap-
 pen*, 75
notion that tendency to process certain
 aspects of language over others are not
 voluntary acts, 22
on presenting one thing at a time, 75
*Processing tense in second language input:
 Lexical cues versus grammatical cues*, 22, 23
verb-object-subject (VOS) word order, 59
verb tense, often marked both
 morphologically and lexically, 26
visual stimuli, 86
vocabulary "giveaway," 84–85
Vygotskian Theory, 5–6
Vygotsky, Lev, 5

Warlpiri, 61
Web-based learning, 91, 102–7. *See also*
 electronic workbook formats
WebCT, 91, 102
 accessing and using, 105t
working memory
 exhausted by lengthy utterances, 14
 limitations, 8, 18, 24, 42

Professor Andrew P. Farley (Ph.D., University of Illinois at Urbana-Champaign) is Assistant Professor of Spanish at University of Notre Dame. Andrew has authored numerous articles and book chapters, and his research has appeared in journals such as *Hispania, Spanish Applied Linguistics, Southern Journal of Linguistics, Estudios de lingüística aplicada,* and in *Processing Instruction,* a volume by Erlbaum Press. Andrew's research interests include input processing in second language acquisition, lexical access in low-level bilinguals, and the effects of focus-on-form instructional interventions. He has presented his research at national and international conferences including American Association of Applied Linguistics (AAAL), Second Language Research Forum (SLRF), American Council on the Teaching of Foreign Languages (ACTFL), American Association of Teachers of Spanish and Portuguese (AATSP), and Form-Meaning Connections in Second Language Acquisition (FMSLA). At Notre Dame, Andrew teaches courses in general linguistics, applied linguistics, second language acquisition, and language teaching methodology, and he serves as Director of the Spanish Language Program.